# play like
# Chet Atkins

Audio

*The Ultimate Guitar Lesson*

CW00822363

## by Andrew DuBrock

To access audio visit:
**www.halleonard.com/mylibrary**

"Enter Code"
2220-2358-1976-5226

Cover photo from Michael Ochs Archives/Getty Images

ISBN 978-1-4803-5389-3

**HAL•LEONARD®**
CORPORATION
7777 W. BLUEMOUND RD. P.O. BOX 13819 MILWAUKEE, WI 53213

Visit Hal Leonard Online at
**www.halleonard.com**

# CONTENTS

# INTRODUCTION

Chet Atkins revolutionized music in more ways than most guitarists ever could. By refining and popularizing a very unique style of alternate-bass guitar picking, he inspired countless guitarists that followed. But as a producer that helped form the foundation of the "Nashville Sound," Atkins influenced the music world as a whole in ways most guitarists couldn't even dream of. In fact, that was never Atkins' aspiration, either. At the heart of it, he was a guitarist first and foremost, and that was where he was most comfortable. This book aims to be the ultimate study on Atkins' playing—from his alternate-bass wizardry to his mastery of harmonics, his vibrato-bar embellishments, and everything in between. We'll take a detailed look at five complete songs, work through 10 more signature passages, study a mountain of licks, look at the essential techniques that form the foundation of his playing, and even take a peak at the stylistic DNA that makes up Chet's unique approach to rolls, harmonics, and other techniques. Once you've gone cover to cover, you'll know how to play many of Atkins' tunes, you'll have the tools to play many more of them, and you'll even know how to apply his unique approach and playing style to your own songs and guitar playing.

*Special thanks to Mark Hanson, Craig Dobbins, and Pat Kirtley for assistance in compiling the information for this book.*

# ABOUT THE AUDIO

To access the audio examples that accompany this book, simply go to **www.halleonard.com/mylibrary** and enter the code found on page 1. This will grant you instant access to every example. The examples that include audio are marked with an audio icon throughout the book.

# GEAR

Here we'll look at Chet Atkins' most prominent instruments and other gear, broken into three subdivisions: the early guitars, the Gretsch years, and the Gibson years. Because Chet's relationship with both Gretsch and Gibson entailed helping design multiple guitar lines, every single iteration of each model he owned is not detailed here. But favorite guitars of any particular model are mentioned when possible.

## Early Guitars

This section will take a look at the favorite guitars he used from the very beginning up through his early stages of success.

### Guitars

- **Sears Roebuck Silvertone flat-top acoustic (circa 1930):** This was Atkins' first guitar. Chet's stepfather, Willie Strevel, brought the guitar home, and his brother Lowell ended up with it. Chet eventually traded his brother an old junk pistol and a year's worth of early morning milking duties for the guitar.

- **Martin Archtop (year unknown):** This was Chet's brother Lowell's guitar, but Chet borrowed it often early on. It was the main guitar he used as staff guitarist for WNOX radio, and he was pictured in some prominent promo photos with the guitar in hand. This was the first guitar onto which he installed a Vibrola tailpiece.

- **Gibson Flat-top (year unknown):** This is the second guitar Atkins owned and was acquired with the help of Aytchie Burns, the bass-playing brother of Jethro Burns.

- **Gibson L-10 (sunburst, 1938):** This guitar was custom built for Les Paul in 1938. Chet's brother, Jimmy, who was playing with Paul at the time, traded for the guitar and gave it to Chet. Atkins used this on the single version of "Main Street Breakdown" and "Galloping on the Guitar," among other things.

- **Gibson L-7 acoustic (sunburst, year unknown):** Prior to 1947, Atkins had been using a DeArmond pickup for amplifying his guitar, but it didn't give the proper balance to his strings. In 1947, he installed P-90 pickups on this L-7, which allowed him to adjust the volume of each string to his liking, and he began playing electric much more often.

- **D'Angelico Excel cutaway (sunburst, 1950):** Much to master luthier John D'Angelico's dismay, Atkins requested this custom guitar be set up for amplification. By the time Atkins was done with it, it had a P-90 pickup at the bridge and a Bigsby pickup at the neck. The first song he recorded with this guitar was "Main Street Breakdown."

### Amps

- **Home-made P.A. (1941):** Chet built his own first "amplifier" in 1941 when he bought an Amperite pickup and made a crude P.A. out of components he ordered.

- **Fender Pro:** This was an early amp that Atkins used with his Gibson L-7.

### Recording

- **RCA 44B and 77 ribbon microphones:** The 44B was used on Atkins' first recording for RCA, and he loved the sound of both the 44B and 77 for recording, claiming he never found anything better.

## The Gretsch Years

In 1953, June Carter knocked Chet's D'Angelico off a stand, and the neck broke off. At this point, the D'Angelico was Atkins' pride and joy, so he tried to have it repaired, but it was never the same until years later when he sent it back to D'Angelico to replace the neck and top. Without his trusty D'Angelico at his side, Chet was forced to look elsewhere for his main axe, and this ushered in the next phase of his guitar-playing years: his affiliation with Gretsch.

In 1954, Atkins met Gretsch representative Jimmie Webster, who began trying to convince Atkins that he should play Gretsch guitars. When Atkins told Webster he didn't like the way their f-holes looked, he didn't like the pickups they used, and he thought they didn't have enough sustain, Webster proposed that Atkins should design his own. Atkins was keen enough on that idea to try it out, so he flew to New York and signed an endorsement deal with Gretsch, setting out to design his own guitars.

Though Chet Atkins' affiliation with Gretsch ended in 1979, his family reestablished the connection after his passing in 2001, and three guitars were re-issued with his namesake: the 6120, the Country Gentleman, and the Tennessee Rose (based on the Tennessean).

## Guitars

- **Gretsch custom Streamliner Special (1954):** This was the first guitar Atkins designed with Gretsch, and it's essentially the prototype of the 6120. While Atkins was integral in helping design the guitar from a sound and playability standpoint, the company took control of the look of the guitar—a bright orange color with belt-buckle tailpiece that Atkins called "hideous."

- **Gretsch Chet Atkins 6120 (1954):** This was Atkins' first signature model guitar, which was based on the custom Streamliner Special he helped design. After the model proved successful, some of the garish cowboy décor was removed, including the cows and cactuses and the large "G" on the lower left bout. Earlier versions of the guitar had a fixed Bigsby vibrato bar installed, the way Atkins liked it, but the company later began using Bigsby arms with a swivel, since customers seemed more keen on having an arm that swiveled.

- **Gretsch Chet Atkins solidbody 6121 (1954):** This guitar came out at the same time as the 6120 and was billed as the "solidbody" version, despite having hollow spaces inside. Unlike the 6120, Atkins didn't have any direct input in the design of this model.

- **Gretsch Country Gentleman (1958):** Another guitar designed with Chet's input, the Country Gentleman was bigger and sturdier than the 6120. The first iteration of the CG came out in 1958, but it was a 1959 model that became Chet's favorite guitar for recording throughout his Gretsch years. By the time this guitar came out, Atkins had convinced the company to include a zero fret and to make smaller f-holes, which were also filled to increase sustain on the Country Gentleman. A double cutaway version was introduced later, which Chet occasionally played in live shows mostly for promotion, but he preferred his older single-cutaway version, which did not have some of the changes and gadgetry introduced by Gretsch that Atkins wasn't keen on.

- **Gretsch Tennessean (1958):** This was the economical version of the Country Gentleman. The company thought they needed to introduce a cheaper model to appeal to consumers, but the Country Gentleman continued to sell as well as the previous 6120.

- **Gretsch Super Chet (1972):** This was a true f-hole hollowbody guitar, which Atkins used on live concerts during the 1970s, though he still preferred his Country Gentleman in the studio. Atkins added an array of switches on the upper bout of his personal Super Chet.

- **Gretsch Deluxe Chet (1972):** This was a cheaper consumer version of the Super Chet released at the same time.

- **Gretsch Super Axe (1976):** A solidbody guitar that Chet helped design, it was equipped with DiMarzio humbuckers. Though it didn't sell as well as the other guitars, Atkins preferred it to the Super Chet and Deluxe Chet models for performing.

- **Hascal Haile nylon-string classical guitar:** Atkins owned several guitars made by Hascal Haile, and they were among his favorites. Haile would later help Atkins design his solid nylon-string Chet Atkins Classical Electric.

- **Juan Estruch nylon-string classical guitar (1959):** Though Atkins was affiliated with Gretsch and electric guitars, he began performing about a half of each show with a nylon-string classical guitar, and this was one of his nylon strings on hand.

- **Manuel Velasquez nylon-string classical guitar (1974):** Another of Chet's classical guitars, this one was a gift from Jorge Morel.

- **Martin 00-40H steel-string acoustic guitar (1920s):** Atkins bought this small-bodied guitar off an acquaintance. It was initially set up with a raised nut for lap-style playing when he bought it, but after having it brought back to a standard setup, it became one of his favorite "sitting and thinking" guitars.

- **Martin 0-21 steel-string acoustic guitar (1845):** This is the oldest guitar Atkins owned. Songwriter Gene MacLellan found it in a pawnshop and gave the guitar to Chet.

- **Martin D-28 steel-string acoustic guitar:** Atkins borrowed this guitar from Harlan Howard in the 1960s, and Howard told him to keep it.

- **Del Vecchio nylon-string resonator guitar:** Atkins bought this from Brazilian guitarist Nato Lima (who wrote "Blue Angel"), and he was given another one by Doyle Dykes.

- **Paul McGill nylon-string resonator guitar:** The Del Vecchio guitars were inconsistently made, so when Atkins wanted another, he had Paul McGill custom build one for him.

- **Gibson Super 400:** Atkins always wanted one of these guitars in his early days but could never afford one. During his years at RCA, someone left this guitar at his office as collateral for borrowed money, but they never claimed it. Atkins forgot whose it was and fell in love with the guitar when he discovered it while cleaning out his office.

## Amps and Effects

- **Standel 25L15:** Atkins traded his Fender Pro amp to Jimmy Day for this amp, which was one of only 50 tube amps built by Bob Crooks. This amp was equipped with a 15" JBL D130 speaker, and it was Atkins' favorite amp by a landslide—especially for recording. He used this amp to record virtually everything from 1954 on, and he liked to mic this amp with the RCA ribbon mics mentioned in the "early guitars" section.

- **Butts EchoSonic:** This amp had a single 15" speaker and was one of Chet's two favorite amps throughout his career (second only to the Standel). Atkins tried out Ray Butts' first one, playing at the Grand Old Opry, and all the guitar players took notice of how great it sounded. Atkins immediately bought the second one Butts made and recorded his first big hit, "Mister Sandman," with it. Atkins also re-wired his guitars so he could get the echo effect only on his bass strings when he plugged into the amp.

- **Echoplex:** This was a tape-based effect unit for live delay that Atkins used.

## Recording

- **Neumann 67 microphone:** Atkins used this condenser mic, along with the RCA ribbon mics mentioned in the previous section, for recording his guitar amps.

- **EV RE-15 microphone:** This was a dynamic microphone Atkins would also use to record his guitars.

## *The Gibson Years*

Gretsch was bought by Baldwin in 1967, and around 1970 the company was moved to Arkansas and consolidated with the Baldwin factory. The skilled employees from the Brooklyn, NY Gretsch factory unfortunately didn't make the move, and the quality of the guitars started to go downhill. Atkins and Fred Gretsch, Jr. managed to convince the company to hire Dean Porter, a Nashville guitar maker, who helped bring the quality upwards, but it was the first sign that the company may not continue to produce the high-quality guitars that Atkins expected. Atkins was a loyal man, though, and despite the inconsistency of Grestch at this point, his long relationship with Fred Gretsch, Jr. kept him affiliated with the company. After Gretsch passed away in 1979, Atkins ended his 25-year relationship with the company.

In the later years of his Gretsch affiliation, Atkins had also worked on an electric nylon-string acoustic prototype with luthier Hascal Haile. He brought the prototype they'd worked on to Gretsch, but the company wasn't interested in the guitar. Once Atkins was no longer affiliated with Gretsch, he approached Gibson with the idea. They'd been after Atkins for years and were interested in developing the guitar with him. Thus began his relationship with Gibson.

## Guitars

- **Hascal Haile custom classical electric (1978):** This solidbody electric nylon-string guitar was built by Hascal Haile (with Atkins' input) and provided the prototype for his Gibson Chet Atkins Classical Electric. It was equipped with a Baldwin Prismatone pickup.

- **Gibson Chet Atkins Classical Electric:** This is the guitar Atkins designed with Gibson based on the custom guitar Hascal Haile built for him.

- **Gibson Country Gentleman (1981):** The second guitar designed and built for Atkins by Gibson, the Gibson Country Gentleman had both Chet and Paul Yandell's input taken into account during the construction process. Atkins felt the final product was better than his earlier Gretsch guitars, due to newer technology and a sturdier design.

- **Gibson Tennessean:** This was Gibson's less expensive version of the Country Gentleman, which came with a fixed tailpiece.

- **Gibson Chet Atkins SST:** This was a steel-string version of the Classical Electric, which was equipped with Lloyd Baggs pickups.

- **Kirk Sand custom semi-acoustic guitar:** This custom guitar acted as a prototype for the Gibson Chet Atkins Studio Classic. It was equipped with a Ray Butts preamp and a Gibson CE pickup.

- **Gibson Chet Atkins Studio Classic:** The SC was Gibson's wide release of a guitar based on the Kirk Sand design. This guitar became one of Atkins' favorite guitars for recording in later years.

- **Gibson Chet Atkins Phasar:** This solidbody guitar looked more like a classic Fender than a traditional Gibson and was equipped with two EMG Fender-style pickups. It had an on-board phaser mounted on the top of the guitar (rather than inside, where it might interfere with the solidbody sound).

- **Gibson Chet Atkins Super 4000:** This guitar was one of a limited edition of 50 archtops built by Gibson in their attempt to make the ultimate archtop guitar.

- **D'Angelico Excel (1948):** This guitar was given to Chet by Jethro Burns before he passed away in 1989.

- **Michael Dunn steel-string acoustic (1995):** This guitar is based on the Selmer-Maccaferri style guitar type that Django Reinhardt played. Atkins liked to use it as a warm-up guitar for performances because it strengthened his hands.

## Amps and Effects

- **MusicMan RD-112:** This amp was one of Chet's favorite touring amps in his later years. However, he always favored his Standel amp for recording.

- **Fender Deluxe:** Atkins and Paul Yandell both had Deluxe amps in custom cabinets made by Paul Riviera.

- **Fender Princeton:** Atkins used this and the Deluxe for live shows prior to his acquiring the MusicMan amp. After he got that amp, he had Yandell sell the Fenders, not wanting to have too many amps lying around.

- **Peavey Special 130:** Atkins used this amp for a little while, but wasn't keen on the heavy tone he got when running his nylon-string guitars through it.

- **Lexicon PCM 42:** Digital delay for live performances.

- **Lexicon Jam Man:** Delay and looping for live performances.

# SONGS

## Mister Sandman
### (Released as a Single, 1954)

Chet Atkins began releasing LPs in 1953, but he'd been recording and releasing singles since his 1946 recording of "Guitar Blues" for Bullet Records. His first single to hit the charts was "Mister Sandman," which climbed all the way to #13 on *Billboard's* "Country Singles" chart in 1955. While many of these early singles were also wrapped into a current or upcoming album, "Mister Sandman" didn't initially find its way onto an LP release, though it's easily found on many compilations nowadays.

### Letter A – Intro

Before we dive into the song itself, check out two key pieces of the transcription that show up at the very beginning: the half note equaling 110 bpm (beats per minute) at the top, and the letter "C" with a slash through it in the time signature. That "C" with a slash through it indicates that you're in *cut time*, which means that you essentially "cut" the time in half; in other words, instead of counting all four beats, you generally just count two beats—"1" on beat 1 and "2" on beat *3* (though people sometimes *do* count out all four beats). An easy way to think about it is that it's just a very fast four beats in a measure, and they're *so* fast that it's often just easier to count two of those beats out. Everything is played just the same as it would be if you counted all four beats. In fact, if you have a drummer, they'll still hit the kick (bass) drum on beats 1 and 3 and the snare on beats 2 and 4. (If they only play one snare hit in a measure, you're in *half time* or playing with a *half-time feel*.) But this cut-time designation is also why the beats per minute are shown for each half note instead of for each quarter note. So, if you set your metronome to 110 bpm to play along, remember that it will only click on beats 1 and 3 of each measure.

As we move into the music itself, Atkins showcases his ability to create lush chordal melodies with close-voiced chords. While he often does this by mixing open strings and fretted notes, here he accomplishes it by stretching his fingers to grab chord shapes spanning up to six frets, allowing these shapes to ring together for the smooth sound heard on record. If you have large hands, this may not pose much of a problem for you. But if your hands are smaller, or if the stretch feels uncomfortable, don't push it! Instead, first try rolling the shapes. For instance, you'll likely be able to hold down the Amaj7 in the first full measure. But in the next measure, as you reach down to grab the second fret with your index finger, allow your pinky to lift off the fretboard (and even your ring finger and middle fingers, if necessary). After you pick the high F♯ note, try to hold it down until you've at least plucked the next note (E), but then feel free to release it as you pick the C♯ note on the third string. Continue this motion by releasing the E note as you pluck the A note on the fourth string, letting at least two strings ring together at any given time.
If you find it too much of a stretch to hold your index and middle fingers down together, we have one more trick up our sleeve—this one stolen from classical piano technique. Here, we'll start playing a note with one finger, and then switch it out to another finger *while the note's still ringing*. For instance, after you play the high F♯ note with your index finger, reach down with either your ring or pinky finger to grab the E note on the fifth fret of the second string. This way, you should be able to let both notes ring together. Then, moments before you want to pluck the *next* note, simultaneously lift your index finger off the fretboard while you trade out your ring (or pinky) finger for the middle finger (it should just slide quickly into place with the note still sounding). Now your hand should be in place to play the rest of the descending run (see photos).

Both of these techniques will still give you a similar ringing effect to Atkins' recording but may save your fingers from tendonitis! If you find that final E9 chord too much of a stretch (in the second ending), you can omit the lowest note without losing the character of the chord, and it will be much easier to grab.

## Letter B – Melody (Key of A)

The melody section that starts at Letter B is a great exercise in playing Chet-style melody over alternate bass (or "Travis Picking"). Focus on letting the upstemmed melody notes ring out while also keeping the downstemmed bass notes thumping and muted by dampening the strings with the palm of your hand. Since the upstemmed melody notes are all played with the fingers while all the downstemmed bass notes are played with the thumb, it's a little easier to visualize how to pull all this off. To keep this easy-to-read and consistent throughout, you may notice one small wrinkle in the notation, and that's because the thumb often comes up and brushes strings that were just played as melody notes. For instance, take a look at measure 11.

As you can see below, the melody and bass notes are nicely separated:

Mister Sandman
Example 1

But if you look closely at the notes, you'll see that your index finger is plucking the third string on beats 1 and 3 and the thumb comes up and brushes across that same string on beats 2 and 4, which essentially cuts off the bottom melody note. So, technically, this is what the notation might look like if that were taken into account:

But this is much more difficult to read! As you can see, the first example clearly separates the melody and bass without too many ties cluttering things up. But because it's written this way, it may throw some people off ("How do I hold out that string and let it ring when I have to pluck it again?!"). Don't worry too much about this. Instead, focus on the melody being separate from the bass and let the melody ring while the bass thumps along, and occasionally interrupts that lower melody note.

Atkins likes to fret the sixth string with his thumb, and he does this often throughout this section. Any time you see a "T" between notation and tab, this indicates when Atkins wraps the thumb around the neck. In many places, like the G♯7 chord in measures 8–9, you may want to resort to a full barre chord, because it's tough to stretch out with your pinky when your thumb is wrapped over the neck. But generally speaking, by fretting with your thumb, you'll have a little more flexibility and movement with your other fingers to grab those other notes (not to mention the fact that you'll get to use an extra finger—your index finger!—which doesn't have to barre). Atkins even uses his thumb to play the notes of some of the nifty bass runs that join several of the chords together—like the run from E up to A in measure 17. Here, he just slides his thumb along, plucking the string as he goes, to fret each note with the thumb as it passes. Incidentally, it also coincides with the shift of the fret hand up to fifth position in measure 18.

There are several places that would be much more difficult—if not impossible—to play without thumb fretting. In measures 32–33, wrapping your thumb around the neck allows you to hold a single shape that includes the open fifth string. Otherwise, you'd have a tough time navigating these measures—especially the pull-off in measure 33, which you'd have to perform while simultaneously removing the barre and slamming that index finger back down on the 10th fret (a knuckle-buster move at best—a disaster, at worst!).

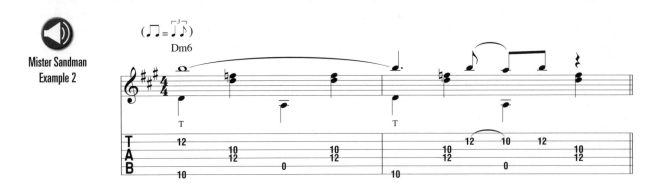

Mister Sandman
Example 2

The other place where thumb fretting really helps out is in measure 35. Here, start out with your thumb *not* fretting while all four fingers grab the chord shape shown: with your middle, index, ring, and pinky fingers grabbing the fifth, fourth, third, and first strings, respectively. Then, leave your ring finger planted on the third string while you roll your hand into place for the next chord. The thumb rolls up over the neck while your index finger should naturally fall into place on the fifth fret of the first string. You'll have a split second longer to get your middle finger in place on the fourth string to hold down that bass note while your pinky grabs the high B note on beat 4.

Mister Sandman
Example 3

## Letter C – Intro Reprise (Key of D)

Once you reach Letter C, you're reprising the intro, but we're not playing the same chords! In fact, we *are* playing the same *chord progression*, but now we've *modulated* to the key of D, which means that we've changed keys from A to D. The I–vi–ii–V progression that initially was Amaj7 (I)–F#m7/A (vi)–Bm7 (ii)–E9 (V) now becomes Dmaj7 (I)–Bm7/D (vi)–Em7 (ii)–A9 (V). The confusing thing here happens when you look at the key signature: three sharps. Hey, we're still in A! The truth is that our stop in the key of D is so short that we don't really acknowledge it, but we *are* briefly in the key of D. However, we just use it as a passing key to move into the key of G, which we do at Letter D.

You've already played this intro progression, but this time you're higher up the neck. These stretches won't we quite as tough, since the frets are closer together up here, but if you have trouble with any of the stretches, use some of the techniques we tried back in Letter A to make things easier to grab.

## Letter D – Melody (Key of G)

Here, Atkins reprises the melody, but now we've modulated into the key of G. The first 16 bars of this section provide a great chance to practice triple stops and also allow you to get familiar with the vibrato bar. For all the *triple stops* (three-note chords, or triads) use the thumb, index, and middle fingers of your picking hand to pluck the strings. All of these triple stops occur on three consecutive strings, but they do shift up and down from the top three strings down one string set to strings 2–4, so make sure you have your thumb and fingers aligned on the proper set before plucking each one:

**Mister Sandman**
**Example 4**

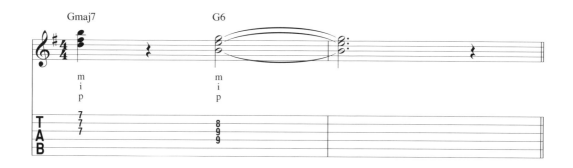

For the vibratoed chords, pluck the chord, grab the bar, and quickly pull it up and release multiple times to get the vibrato effect that alternates between the original pitches and notes *higher* than the chord. For the dip in measures 49–50, however, you'll need to grab the bar (or simply plant your palm on top of it) and push *down* to bend the notes downward. Use your ear to let you know when you've gone down a half step (the distance of one fret). You can always check yourself by releasing the bar and playing the full chord down one fret to give yourself a reference point. Once your hand knows exactly how far to push the bar, you'll be able to dip the bar *before* plucking the strings, creating a scoop up into the chord from a half step below—a technique not used in this tune, but one that Atkins used to great effect with tunes like "Trambone."

For the second half of this section, Atkins breaks chordal shapes up into their individual notes for a serious arpeggio workout. Here, again, he uses three-string chordal shapes and plays them with his thumb, index, and middle fingers, shifting up or down a string set to pluck whichever group he's focusing on at the time, like this:

**Mister Sandman**
**Example 5**

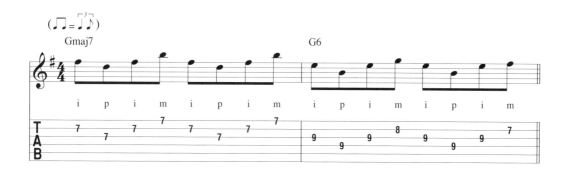

At Letter E, Atkins again reprises the intro, this time in the key of C. Unlike Letter C—where we briefly passed through the key of D on our way to the key of G—at Letter E, we play our intro in C and park in that key for the rest of the song.

## Letter F – Melody (Key of C)

Chet plays the melody again up in the key of C, but he uses very similar shapes to those used at Letter B. The main adjustment here is fretting the bass notes for the C chords (since many of the A chord bass notes were played on the open strings).

The most difficult part of this section involves some tricky thumb fretting near the end of the song. The Fm6 chord in measures 106–107 is quite difficult. Here, you'll have to fret over the neck with your thumb to grab *both* the fifth and sixth strings at the eighth fret, like this:

Not only is this stretch difficult, but the angle of your fingers—which are further up the fretboard than your thumb—make this nearly impossible for mortals! Alternatively, you could try this barre fingering:

The other difficult passage falls at the very end of the song when he slides a 9#11 chord shape down the fretboard in measures 110–112. This chord shape is a certifiable finger twister any way you play it, but Atkins solved the problem by wrapping his thumb over the neck and playing the bass note with his thumb on the fifth string again. If you haven't tried this before, it's not quite as crazy as it sounds—especially if your guitar neck isn't terribly thick. Fret the bass note on the fifth string with your thumb and then barre across the top four strings with your index finger one fret back. Finally, place your middle and ring fingers on the second and third strings at the same fret as the thumb, like this:

If you listen carefully to the original recording, you can actually hear Atkins slapping his thumb onto the fretboard on beats 1 and 3 of each measure; you hear a ghost note down on the sixth string of each chord—the low fifth of each chord—where his thumb lands:

Mister Sandman
Example 6

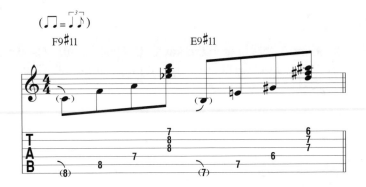

For the final chord in the song, unwrap your hand from your guitar's neck and play the C6 by fretting the C note with your index finger and barring across the fifth fret with your ring finger. If you need some extra support to get all those barred notes to sound, feel free to experiment with your pinky and middle fingers to achieve enough pressure.

# MISTER SANDMAN

Lyric and Music by Pat Ballard

Mister Sandman
Full Song

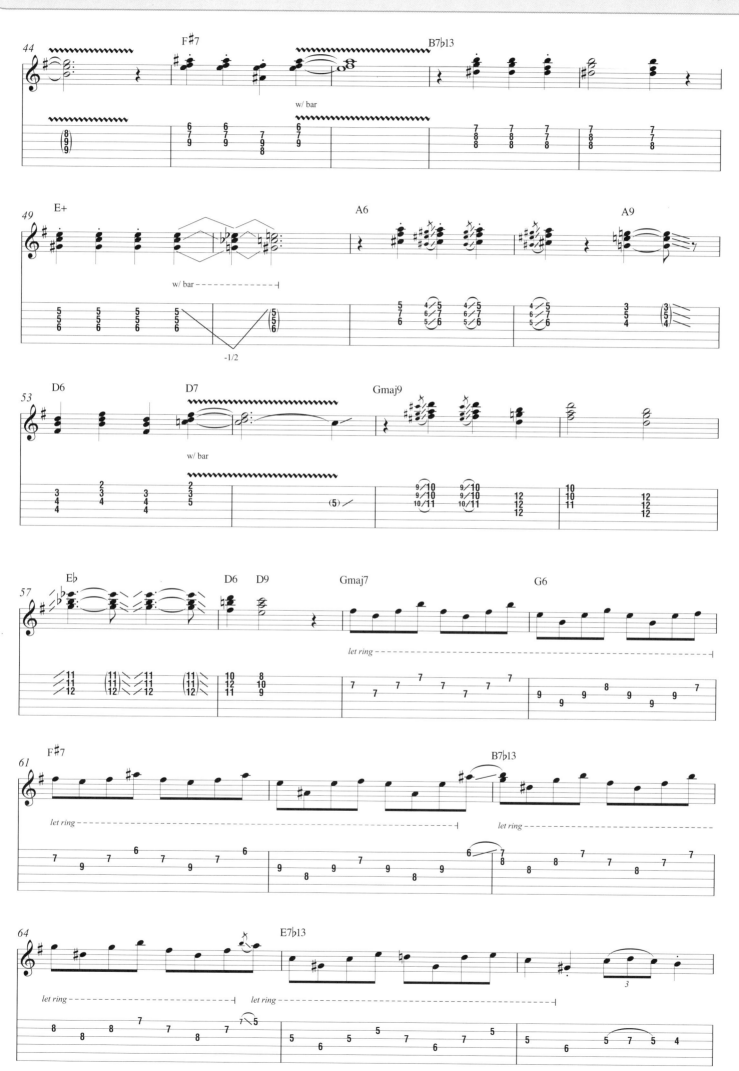

# Yakety Axe
## (*More of That Guitar Country*, 1965)

"Yakety Axe" was Chet Atkins' take on a contemporary hit of the time—saxophonist Boots Randolph's "Yakety Sax." Randolph's original version became known to the masses through its inclusion on *The Benny Hill Show*, and Atkins' version brought him plenty of success, too. Released in 1965 as a single, the tune went on to reach #4 on *Billboard's* Hot Country chart—the highest mark of any of his tunes on that chart. The track was also included on *More of That Guitar Country*, and the song helped push the record to #4 on *Billboard's* Country album charts, as well.

Atkins later recorded a slower version as a duet with Mark Knopfler on their 1990 release, *Neck and Neck*, and Merle Travis wrote some lyrics for this later version, which Atkins sang. In this lesson, we'll take a look at Atkins' classic original cut of the tune.

## Letter A

"Yakety Axe" is played at the burning tempo of 120 bpm for each *half note*! That's because we're in *cut time* (see the performance notes for "Mister Sandman" for more on cut time). This tune is a great study in Chet Atkins' single-note playing, and he kicks things off in style with a very gradual bend in measure 4, which he matches in pitch on the first string in the next measure. Similar to a *unison bend*, which involves two notes sounding simultaneously, this is a great way to practice your bending technique because you've got a reference pitch right there for your bend—the unison note on the next string. But the trick with this particular bend is that Atkins plays the first note on beat 2, starts bending, and doesn't reach his destination until beat 1 of the next measure! Most of us pickers are used to bending immediately up to a note (or at least fairly quickly), so it can take a bit of practice to nail this gradual bend. You don't want to bend so quickly that you reach your target before the next measure, and you don't want to take so long to get there that you have to yank it up quickly at the end. Instead, you want a smooth transition all the way from the plucked note to the target note. Atkins used his ring finger for the bend, adding his middle finger in for extra support, but if you're more comfortable playing this with your pinky (with your ring *and* middle fingers for extra support), by all means play it that way. Either way you play it, adding an extra finger or two for support will help this precision bend rise at just the right rate. If it's not naturally falling into place, try looping it to get the hang of it. Start by repeating the bend and the unison note on the first string, just to make sure you're bending up to that target note. Your ears will tell you when it's right:

Yakety Axe
Example 1

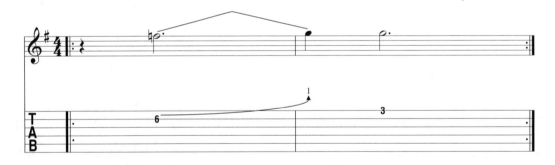

Once you've practiced that a while, your fingers should be starting to get the hang of what it feels like. And when the target note is firmly ingrained in your head, you can speed up your progress by looping just the bend:

Yakety Axe
Example 2

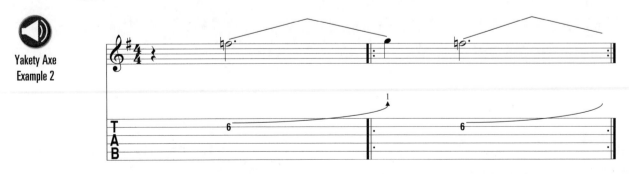

Throughout the tune, Atkins plucks the lead lines by alternating with his thumb and index finger. In general, he plucks most every note on a beat with his thumb, using his index finger to pick the notes on each eighth-note subdivision that falls between the beats. This seems fairly intuitive, once you try it out:

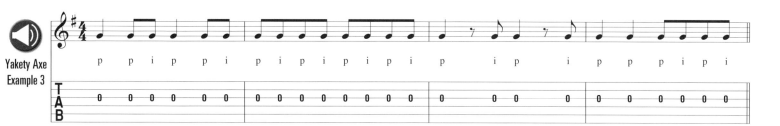

Yakety Axe
Example 3

Now try this picking out with the opening phrase. You'll start with the bend, plucking it with your thumb. Once you finish the bend, the next note (the G on string 1) is virtually the only note played on the beat that Chet picks with his index finger. After this note, he immediately begins alternating between his thumb and index finger to close out the phrase:

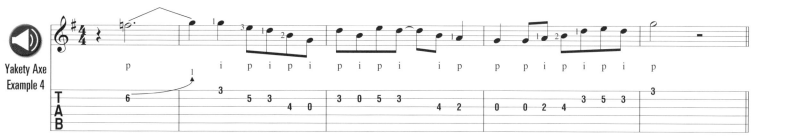

Yakety Axe
Example 4

Aside from the first F natural note, the entire first line of the song is built using the G major pentatonic scale (G–A–B–D–E), but check out how he uses both the open B string and the fretted B note (string 3, fret 4) to streamline the fingering, accessing whichever one is the most convenient at any given point:

G Major Pentatonic Scale

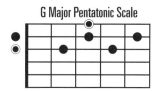

The second line of the song is nearly identical for the first two measures but changes in the third measure, as the chord changes to D. Here, the melody utilizes a full G major scale via the addition of the F♯ note, which highlights the harmony of the D chord (F♯ is the 3rd of D).

In the third line phrase (measures 12–16), Atkins eschews the bending for the slinkier sound of sliding, and he uses his ring finger again to zip from the sixth-fret F up to the eighth-fret G. This momentarily throws you out of position, so you'll have to move quickly to get your hand back down the fretboard in time for your index finger to grab the G note back at the third fret, first string. In measure 15, you repeat this move down on the second and third strings over the C chord. Here, the tuning of the G and B strings makes things slightly easier, since you only have to shift back two frets to grab the C note with your index finger.

At the end of measure 16, Atkins plucks the F note and slides that up all the way from the sixth fret to the 12th, followed by slides back and forth between the 10th and 12th frets for an incredibly slinky line. Don't worry too much about precisely articulating that F note at the beginning. The destination note, B, is most important here, so if you simply pluck the string while sliding up the fretboard (and keeping contact with the string), you'll get the desired effect. The notes to pay attention to here are the B and A notes that you're sliding back and forth between. This is actually pretty tricky to perform cleanly. In fact, Atkins would sometimes cheat here in live performances, and you can too, if it makes your life easier. His trick was to only perform the first slide—the one from the sixth to the 12th fret—and then fret the B and A notes with his middle and ring fingers, respectively, picking each one. He also sometimes modified the lick slightly by playing an A♯ note instead of an A natural. You may want to try this as a slide, too, since it's easier to slide that one-fret distance than the original two-fret distance at the burning tempo of the song.

Yakety Axe
Example 5

Atkins closes this section with a funky line in measure 19, highlighted by the tritone interval of E–B♭. Occasionally referred to as the "devil's tone" (especially in classical music), the *tritone's* diminished 5th interval (or augmented 4th) is what gives it such a discordant sound. Atkins uses a B♭ here to create the tritone, and B♭ is the ♭3rd of G, which isn't part of the G major or major pentatonic scales with which the opening phrases were crafted. This ♭3rd, along with the ♭7th, are borrowed from the G minor (or minor pentatonic) scale, and Atkins sprinkles them more heavily into the mix from measures 16–19 to add some spice to these lines. The minor-to-major 3rd lick in measure 18 is particularly popular in bluegrass lines and is even found in the famous bluegrass "G run."

## Letter B

The next section borrows heavily from the first, so you already know how to play three quarters of this material! The only new phrase here begins at the tail end of measure 24 and runs through measure 28. Use your ring finger to slide from the E note all the way up to the B note at the 12th fret of string 2. This is a big slide, and while the first note is more important than the quick sliding note we looked at back in measure 16, don't worry about articulating that note for longer than a split second. In fact, as soon as your pick hits the string, start sliding on up to that 12th fret. Once you're up in the 10th position, your fingers are in a convenient one-finger-per-fret box shape to grab those 10th- and 12th-fret notes with your index and ring fingers, respectively. Simply slide this same one-finger-per-fret formation down to the seventh and fifth positions in the next two measures for the licks lower down. All you have to add in is your middle finger, which grabs the note in between—that eighth-fret G note in measure 26 and the sixth-fret F natural in measure 27. From here on out, everything's identical to the previous section (Letter A).

## Letter C

Letter C kicks off with a similar bend to the last two sections, but here we're up at the 11th fret because we've abruptly jumped into a different key: C major. The four measures that begin this section are a direct quote from "Entrance of the Gladiators" by Czech composer Julius Fucik. That name likely won't ring any bells for you, but if you play the passage or listen to the recording, you'll recognize it immediately as the "theme" that has since become synonymous with clowns at the amusement park. Atkins also occasionally quoted another tune in live performances ("The Girl I Left Behind"), but not on this original recording of "Yakety Axe." The quoting of these songs—"Entrance of the Gladiators" in particular—accentuates the playfulness of both "Yakety Axe" and Atkins. This isn't one of his serious tunes! Atkins often played a somewhat funky fingering for the second and third measures of this passage (measures 38–39) in live performances where he planted his index finger at the eighth fret, sliding down to grab each note at the seventh fret, like this:

Yakety Axe
Example 6

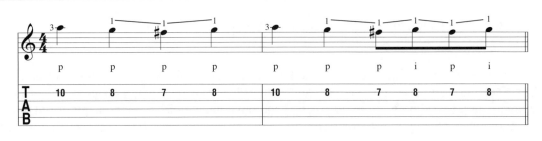

You may find this a bit unwieldy, especially in the third measure of the phrase (measure 39 of the transcription), where he slides back and forth several times between frets 7 and 8. If so, you can leave your hand "shifted" down to that seventh fret in the second measure of the lick and play the next measure using one finger per fret, like this:

Yakety Axe
Example 7

In measure 41, Atkins plays a version of the previously mentioned bluegrass G run, here transposed up to C. Again, Atkins shifts slightly back and forth between seventh and eighth position to take advantage of his dominant index and ring fingers, like this:

Yakety Axe
Example 8

At measure 43, Atkins transposes the D7 lick from measure 11 up to G7—played here at the tenth position. Then, in measures 45–48, he really digs in to a set of percussive triplet licks to bring the energy level up as he heads into the final phrases of the section. Here, Atkins uses a quick, rolling p-i-m-p picking pattern, bringing his thumb all the way up to the first string to add extra emphasis to those high notes, like this:

Yakety Axe
Example 9

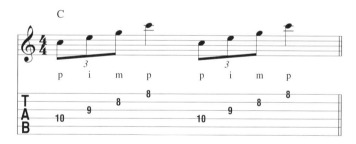

Not only does this add extra punch to the high notes that complete each arpeggio, but it also keeps your thumb playing on all of the beats. However, if you find your thumb and fingers tripping over each other, you can always use your ring finger on the first string, creating a p-i-m-a pattern, which you might find easier (especially if you commonly use that ring finger for picking.):

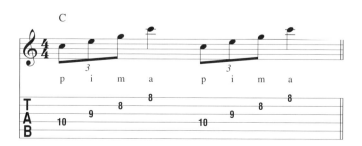

Measures 49 and 51 are similar to the licks he played in measures 41–42, though here they're split apart with a C major-scale run wedged in between, over the G7 measure.

## Letter D

Atkins takes a little breather at Letter D, letting the energy back off a bit for a little contrast. The theme of this section is "economy of motion." Atkins parks his hand in third position here and doesn't move it until measure 61 (eight full measures). Plant your ring finger on the fifth fret of the third string and reach up with your pinky to grab those fifth-fret A notes on string 1. That leaves your index finger ready for the third-fret G notes on string 1 and your middle finger awaiting the fourth-fret B notes on string 3 that arrive in measure 59. For your picking hand, continue alternating between your thumb and index finger on the third string, but use your middle finger for all of the notes that occur on the first string. Here are the first eight measures with fret- and pick-hand fingerings:

Yakety Axe
Example 10

At measure 61, slide your hand up to fifth position, using your index finger for all of the fifth-fret C notes on the third string for the next three measures. Reach up with your pinky for the eighth-fret C note on the first string, and use your ring and middle fingers for the notes on the sixth and fifth frets on string 1, respectively. In measure 64, slide up to the eighth fret, using your index and middle fingers on the third and first strings, respectively. This will put you in position for the final phrase of this passage. Don't worry if all those fret and string numbers made your head spin! Here's a visual, so you can easily see which fingers to place where:

Yakety Axe
Example 11

Atkins then closes out this section with the same set of licks with which he finished Letter C.

## Letter F

At this point, you've pretty much learned the entire song! Chet lays out for Letter E while the band strums backup chords behind the harmonica, and the first 15 measures of Letter F are identical to Letter B. The *next* 16 measures (96–111) are identical to Letter A, and the only thing left to learn is the ending lick. Atkins ends with another lighthearted quote—this time using the "shave and a haircut" lick in measure 113 to go out with a chuckle.

# YAKETY AXE

Words by Merle Travis
Music by Boots Randolph and James Rich

# Dizzy Strings
## (Released as a Single, 1948)

Chet Atkins originally released "Dizzy Strings" way back in 1948 as a single. Since then, the tune has shown up on multiple compilations, including *Galloping Guitar: The Early Years* (1993) and *Legacy* (2007). The tune shows that Atkins was already a fully formed virtuoso by the late '40s, featuring many of his signature techniques: dazzling pull-off licks, rolls, up-the-neck licks mixed with open strings, a little vibrato-bar diving, and the sound Atkins is most associated with—his alternate-bass fingerpicking with syncopated melodies on top.

## Letter A

"Dizzy Strings" begins with a flurry of notes, as Chet whips through some rapid-fire triplet pull-offs on the top two strings. Align your fingers over the first four frets, with one finger per fret (first finger = first fret, etc.), and you'll be perfectly set to take off. Each pull-off requires a two-finger combination, and your ring/middle combination is by far the most used here. In fact, there's only one use of anything else—the index/middle hammer-on combo at the end of measure 2 (which also happens to be the only hammer-on combination, as well). Here's the passage with those fingerings noted:

Dizzy Strings
Example 1

Developing comfort and fluidity on these pull-offs (and the one set of hammer-ons) can take some time. Try practicing these exercises for a while, which apply the patterns up and down every string, alternating between hammer-ons and pull-offs so that you get equal practice with each for every two-fret combination (frets 1–2 and 2–3). The first two exercises focus on each isolated finger combination. If you want a real workout, try putting the two together, as in the third exercise!

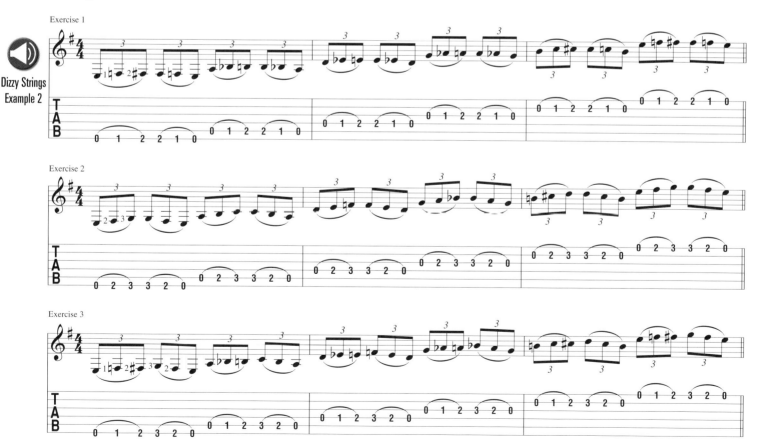

Dizzy Strings
Example 2

The notes of this passage come from the "composite blues scale," which is a mixture of the major pentatonic scale and what is commonly called the "blues scale."

**Dizzy Strings Example 3**

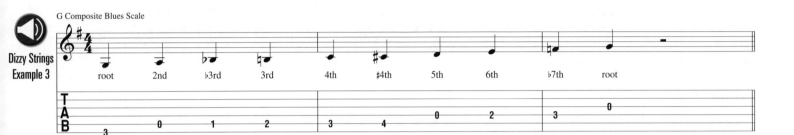

In the context of this passage, though, there's a brightness that comes from that blue ♯4/♭5th tone, since it's essentially used as the only 4th in the passage (aside from the brief chromatic hammer-on run up the second string at the end of measure 2). This contrasts heavily with the darker sound of the ♭3rd (B♭) on the third string. In reality, though, rather than thinking too heavily about the theoretical end of things, it's likely that Atkins was simply picking out target tones he liked and then plugging them into an easy fingering. His fingers were likely gravitating towards the same 3-2-0 pattern on both strings, his ear was focusing on the 5th (D) and 3rd (B) on the second string and the ♭3rd (B♭) and root (G) on the second string, and the cool scale was simply the result.

## Letter B

At Letter B, Atkins uses one of his favorite roll patterns to navigate a G6–C9–Am7–D9 chord progression. The roll pattern cycles through a three-note p–i–m sequence five times. The trick here is that he uses his thumb (p) and index finger (i) exclusively on the fourth and third strings, respectively. But he uses his middle finger (m) to alternate between the second and first strings, like this:

**Dizzy Strings Example 4**

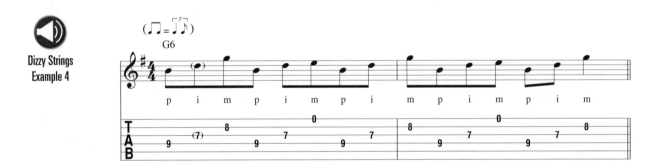

Now, when you see all the notes and tablature filling up the page, this phrase actually looks a lot more complicated than it really is. Atkins is really just fretting chord shapes and applying the picking pattern to those shapes. If we look at the shapes themselves, this section becomes much less intimidating. Here are the four shapes:

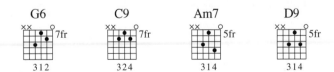

The syncopation created by the three-note pattern in 4/4 time can also easily trip you up. So if you have trouble integrating all these things at once, let's work up to it. First, we'll simply use triplets for the pattern, which will get rid of the syncopation, allowing us to play four sets of triplets in each measure. And we'll practice it with our middle finger playing only on the second string:

Dizzy Strings
Example 5

Next, we'll try that out again, but this time we'll only pluck notes on the first string with that middle finger:

Dizzy Strings
Example 6

Now comes the fun part! Here, we'll start by playing a full measure (four triplets) with our middle finger on the second string and then alternate that with another full measure where our middle finger jumps up to the first string. We'll gradually work up to things by shifting between strings every two triplets and then finish by alternating on every triplet, just like the phrases in the song:

Dizzy Strings
Example 7

Next, we'll get rid of our triplets and shift back to the syncopated eighth notes. Since the pattern is under our fingers, our body can now get a good feel for this syncopation. Tap along with your foot to keep the beat and notice how that means different notes of the three-note pattern are accented every time you play it. Also check out how, if we just keep playing, it actually takes *three* measures to cycle back through to where the thumb starts beat 1 again—not the two measures that Atkins plays in "Dizzy Strings":

**Dizzy Strings Example 8**

This is why Atkins cuts things short in the second measure, holding out that final note for a quarter note. It turns the pattern into a more common two-measure pattern:

**Dizzy Strings Example 9**

After he finishes the roll pattern up, he finishes Letter B off with a nice little lick reminiscent of Gypsy jazz icon Django Reinhardt. Here Atkins is showing off one of his many favorite influences. After all the hammer-ons and pull-offs in the intro, the fretting hand part should be a breeze. And for your picking hand, there are several ways you can play this passage. You could hold your index finger and thumb together and use the thumbpick like a flatpick (or if you don't play with a thumbpick, you could hold them together and use the index finger in place of a flatpick). Alternatively, you could simply alternate between the thumb and index fingers to pick the notes, using your thumb on the beats and your index finger to pick the notes in between. Atkins would often switch between the first and last method of picking out lead lines, depending on how fast the licks were, and this line falls neatly in the middle, so either way should work well:

**Dizzy Strings Example 10**

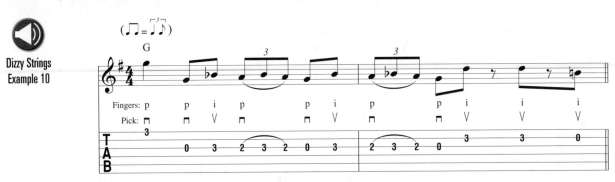

## Letter C

Letter C begins with Atkins riffing on his Django-inspired lick for four full measures. Then, at measure 18, he swings even further into Gypsy jazz territory with a four-measure passage that sounds as though it came straight from a Parisian club in the 1930s. It starts with an ascending arpeggio line—a staple of Hot Club-era licks—that morphs from an A7 arpeggio into a C♯ diminished arpeggio midway through the line. At the top, a little hammer-and-pull move to and from B♭ (the ♭9th) adds a flourish before another A7 arpeggio descent in measure 19. Next, a quick chromatic move downward leads to the following D7 arpeggio at the beginning of the next measure. *Chromatic* is simply a term used for notes that are out of a chord or progression's key; it's the counterpart for *diatonic*, which means that the notes *do* come from the underlying chord or key. If that all sounds complicated, it's good to just know that "chromatic" is often used when notes move several half steps in a row, and that's what happens here as we move through the notes A–A♭–G.

Up through this A7 arpeggio, you can access virtually everything from fifth position. Start one fret below—at the fourth fret—and use your index and pinky fingers for the C♯ and E notes on the fifth string. Then, slide up one fret and use one finger per fret with your index finger at the fifth fret. Reach down with that index finger to grab the other lone note on the fourth fret (the F♯ at the beginning of measure 20). Midway through measure 20, however, we depart from this position with the nifty hammer/pull lick that moves down the fretboard. Use your index and ring fingers on the fifth and seventh frets, respectively, and then simply slide that down a fret for the next hammer/pull combination, sliding down again to grab the third-fret D note with your index finger. This is another slinky chromatic line that pays homage to Django and his Hot Club sounds. Here's that whole combination with pick-hand fingerings in place to help you navigate all the way through:

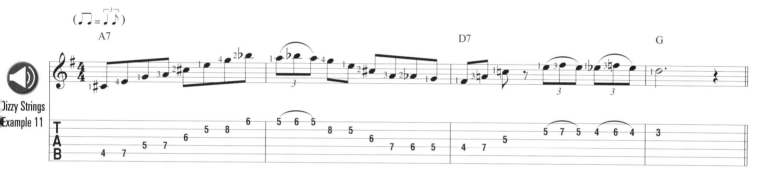

Dizzy Strings
Example 11

Atkins closes out this section with a reprise of the roll pattern from Letter B—the main theme of the song.

## Letter D

Chet begins Letter D with a bending lick that would define a decade of rockers to come in the 1950s, like Chuck Berry. Many folks play this lick by barring across the top two strings at the third fret with the index finger while using their ring finger to perform the bend underneath at the sixth fret. You could use your pinky for the bend, but the ring finger is considerably stronger, and without the help of that index finger for the bend, it's a good deal easier to use that stronger digit. You can, however, back it up with your middle finger.

Now while many rockers would let these notes ring together, Atkins actually doesn't do this, which makes the lick a little tougher. Instead of being able to leave that index finger firmly planted throughout the lick, you'll need to lift it ever so slightly after each note that it frets, so that you can dampen the note before articulating the next one. *Fret-hand muting* like this is invaluable in helping you shape your phrases, since you can make notes ring (or not ring) for as long as you want to.

The "color tone" in this lick is the tasty ♭5th (or ♯4th), which is considered one of the "blue" tones, along with the ♭3rd and ♭7th. In fact, this particular bluesy note is the *only* addition to the minor pentatonic scale that changes it into what many people call the "blues scale," which we briefly mentioned in the Intro section (Letter A):

Dizzy Strings
Example 12

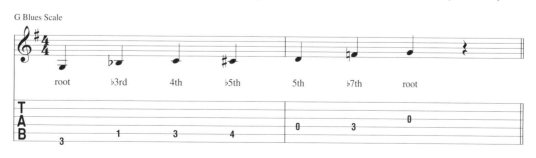

At measure 32, Atkins descends from the high G note, hitting that blue ♭5th again on his way to another hammer/pull move in measure 33 that's similar to the earlier move back at the beginning of Letter C. But this time, we're up a scale tone and operating out of the third and fifth frets, instead of the second and third frets.

After ascending a G major pentatonic scale (with the added ♭3rd for spice), Atkins closes this phrase with a tasty half-step bend up to the ♭7th in measure 34 and several more quotations of our newfound hammer/pull combo in measures 36–37.

At this point, we run headfirst into another one of Atkins' signature patterns—the melodic lick alternating between an open string and fretted notes up the neck—which takes us from measure 38 all the way through measure 43. At first listen, the syncopated three-note pattern here reminds us of the roll patterns we played earlier in the song. But here, the technique is quite a bit different. (And the sound is actually, too, except for the syncopation; here, things don't ring together the way they do during the rolls.) Instead of a roll, Atkins plucks this out by alternating between his thumb and index finger for each note. This is a bit tricky, since his thumb occasionally "overlaps" his index finger by sometimes playing the higher string. Isolate the first two measures and slow it down to get the hang of it, if you need to. Here's the picking pattern shown for those first two measures:

*Dizzy Strings*
*Example 13*

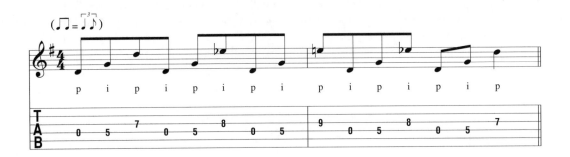

## Letter E

At Letter E, Atkins promptly does something that we don't expect from superhero guitarists—he makes a mistake! The truth is that *everyone* makes mistakes sometimes, but for a guitarist of Atkins' caliber they usually go by so quickly, and he *recovers* so quickly, that you never notice it. What Atkins *intends* to do at the beginning of Letter E is start playing a roll pattern that cycles through a C9–G6–A9–D9 chord progression (playing two measures of each chord) that lasts all the way through measure 53. But he doesn't quite get his hand in place at the beginning, and that's why there are a few muffled notes as he adjusts. Of course, that adjustment is so quick that by the middle of the first measure, he's already plucking out his roll, and one barely notices he missed a beat. Just so you have a point of reference, here's what Atkins intended to play in measures 46–47.

*Dizzy Strings*
*Example 14*

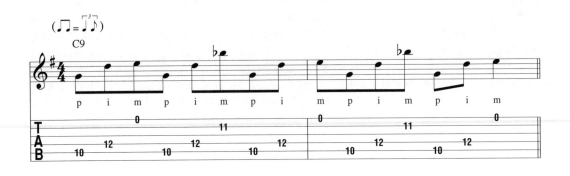

Once you see the notes on the page (and the tablature on the strings), it's apparent he's just starting the same pattern that he keeps up for eight measures. Use a p-i-m pattern throughout the full eight measures—one of Chet's favorite roll patterns. One of the more difficult aspects of this pattern is the stretch between the index and middle fingers of your picking hand. For the first roll, you have to skip *two* strings between these fingers and then reach down with your middle finger for the second roll to grab a string lower (now there's only one string separating your index and middle fingers). If you have trouble nailing this roll at first, try repeating the roll until you get the hang of it:

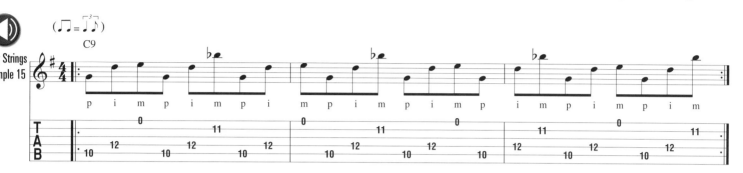

Just like the roll pattern at Letter B, this one takes three measures to cycle through. Once you have it under your fingers, you can go back to Atkins' two-measure version, which holds out the last beat in the second measure. You can cycle through this pattern a few times to practice, too. (It just doesn't quite give you the same repetition since it stops after every second measure.)

Once you have the roll down, it's time to put the eight-measure pattern together. If you can get your hand up to the 10th fret quickly enough to start this passage on the downbeat (after playing the previous two measures in the song), you're doing great! Of course, if you can't get up there in time, you're in fine company, too.

At measure 54, Atkins shifts down to seventh position to highlight the G chord with this G6 chord shape on the top three strings:

But he adds some character to this chord by first playing the shape *down* a half step and bending the first two strings up a half step to reach the notes of a G chord. Then, he pops up into the shape in measure 55 and continues into measure 56 with some more nifty embellishment with the vibrato bar. Here, he highlights the C7 chord with 5th (G) and 7th (B♭) degrees on the top two strings, but executes a precision pre-bent dip with the bar to make the notes start a quarter tone flat, and then scoops up into tune on the downbeat of measure 56—a great effect. A few more single notes, a tasty held half-step bend, and some revisited licks from earlier in the song in measures 60–61 close out this section.

## Letters F–H

Throughout Letters F and G, Chet lays out while the fiddle and accordion take turns soloing. At H, he picks up themes from the C section and latter portion of the B section, mixing them together in slightly new ways. Then, heading into measure 92, Atkins quotes the intro of the song with a flurry of mostly pull-off runs down at the nut (with an occasional hammer-on or two). But, unlike the intro—which runs along the second and third strings—here, Atkins accesses the same fingerings along the first and second strings. This spells out the more straightforward G Lydian mode (instead of the composite blues scale found in the intro):

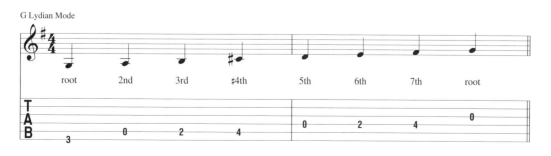

He comes out of this run by shifting to a darker sounding G minor pentatonic lick (G–B♭–C–D–F) in measure 94 that quickly makes a right turn back into bright Lydian territory with the hammer/pull combo on beat 4. Again, with the exception of the G minor pentatonic lick, this set of licks is likely more borne out of fretboard fingering shapes and note targeting than a conscious desire to mine the depths of the composite blues scale or Lydian mode.

Atkins closes out the section with some embellished arpeggios that highlight the backing chords—a C7 arpeggio with the added 6th (A) over C7, a D6 arpeggio over the D7 chord, and a G major arpeggio for the G chord. Note the little wobble he gives to this passage with the pre-bent vibrato-bar dive in measure 97 and the vibrato on the final G note.

## Letter I

At Letter I, Atkins starts his signature alternate-bass fingerpicking for the first (and only) time in the song. The C9 chord shape is easy enough. Fret a barred C major chord at the eighth fret, remove your pinky from the fourth string (which adds the ♭7th tone underneath with your barred index finger), and just replace that pinky finger on the first string at the 10th fret:

But the G6/9 chord in measure 104 is tough to grab as Chet does. Relying on his rather large hands, he frets both bottom strings with his thumb.

If your thumb simply can't wrap around the neck that far, don't push it! You don't want to damage your hands, and there are always ways you can create nearly the same thing. For instance, here you could fret the bottom two strings with your middle and ring fingers, barre the third and fourth strings with your index finger, and use your pinky to barre the top two strings, as seen in the adjacent photo.

Unfortunately, this isn't a picnic in the park, either. If your hand is too small for both of these shapes, the best way to go is to simply leave out the sixth string, fretting the fifth string with your middle finger, barring the third and fourth strings with your index finger, and either fretting the top two strings with your ring and pinky fingers or barring those two notes with your ring finger, as seen in the adjacent photo.

In measure 106, Atkins picks out a well-placed drop-2 A7 voicing with the 5th (E) on the first string. Drop-2 seventh-chord voicings are four-string chords built on a consecutive set of four strings, and they're great for alternate-bass fingerpicking—especially when you have an open bass note on the fifth or sixth string (or both). You can build a drop-2 voicing from any note of a chord on the first string starting with that chord tone on top. The general concept for building these chords is that you want to have each chord tone in ascending order on consecutive strings, but the problem with the guitar is that arranging notes in this order requires a difficult (and sometime impossible) stretch. So, you *drop* the note on the second string *two* strings down to the fourth string ("drop 2"), as shown in the following example:

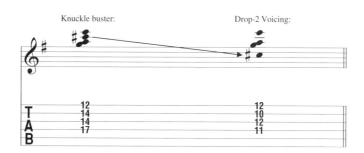

In measures 108–110, Atkins superimposes a descending series of chords over the D chord, which are all triads from the harmonized G major scale—D, C, Bm, and Am. He then comes to rest on the same bent dyad in measure 110 that he used back in measure 54. In measure 111, he alternates between two dyads that interlock to create a jazzy G6 sound, then riffs on several licks found prominently at the beginning of Letter D and the end of Letter E. Note here, though, how he holds down *two* strings with his index finger for the triplet lick to get the ringing dyad sound over the slinky triplet figure. (Also check out his quick shift from playing the fourth-fret B note—the 3rd—on the first triplet to the fifth-fret C note—the 4th.)

## Letter J

At Letter J, Atkins and the fiddle player alternate breaks during each eight-measure section, with the fiddler kicking things off, getting the first six bars while Chet takes the final two bars. He closes both sections with the flurry of triplet pull-offs used in the intro (Letter A) and Letter H.

## Letter K

Chet continues his flurry of triplet pull-offs into Letter K, playing the cascading line all the way into measure 139. In previous sections, we looked at how Atkins' fingers likely "did the walking" to play pull-off shapes that were easy to translate up and down the fretboard while also targeting just a few key notes. Letter K shows some extra thought going on behind the scenes as he subtly adjusts these patterns to the underlying chords. As he comes into Letter K from the G chord, he's using the same pattern on the top two strings: frets 3, 2, and 0. But when he hits the C7 chord at Letter K, he plays the 3–2–0 pattern on the first and third strings, but adds his index finger in on the second string to play a 3–2–1 pattern. This highlights the C note at the end of each of those triplets, which is the root of the C7 chord—a subtle but neat trick to adapt to the underlying chords. In measure 136, he switches back to the original pattern over the G chord again but adapts again to play the pattern over an A7 chord in measure 138. Here, he shifts to a 2–1–0 pattern to especially highlight key chord tones on the first and third notes of the triplet: the E (5th), C♯ (3rd), A (root), and G (7th). The pattern also accentuates several colorful extensions: the jazzy 13th (F♯) and 9th (B). At the end of measure 139, Atkins brushes through an Am chord at the fifth fret that hammers into a descending G major scale (G–A–B–C–D–E–F♯) over the D7 chord. But to go out with a little color, he slides into the C♯ note at the end (the bright ♯4 sound from the Lydian mode we looked at earlier in the song).

Atkins backs off for the next six measures as the fiddle player takes a final break. Then, Chet goes out with a bang, alternating hammer-on and pull-off triplets in a descending pattern down through the strings. On beat 4 of measure 148, notice how he shifts his hand up one fret so that he can nail the 3rd (B) on the downbeat of the next measure. This means that he ends up playing a 4–3–2 pattern with his ring, middle, and index finger in that order. After a final hammer-on line on string 6, Chet rakes out a 12th-fret natural harmonic, which he embellishes with a slight dip and vibrato from the bar.

# DIZZY STRINGS

## By Chet Atkins

*Chord symbols reflect overall harmony.

End Rhy. Fig. 1

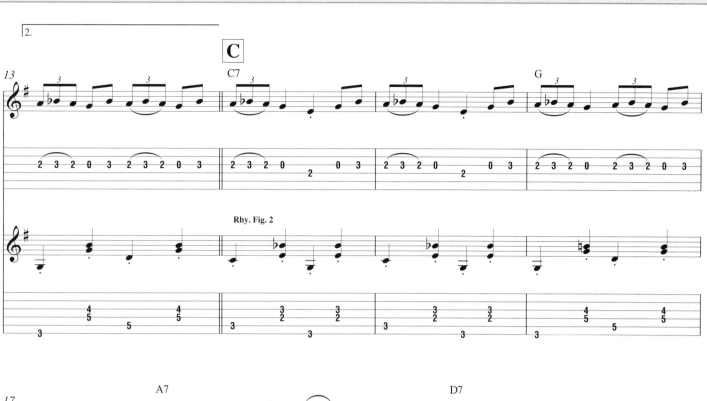

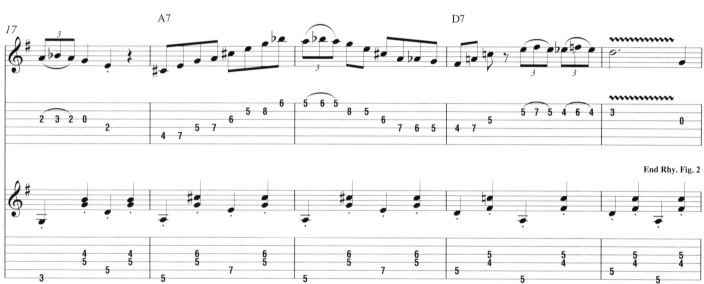

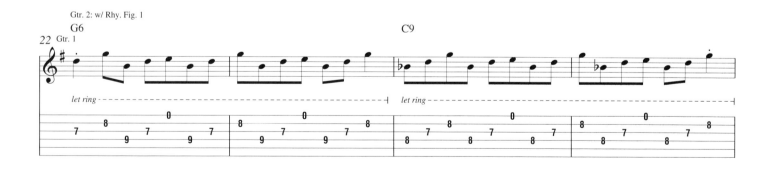

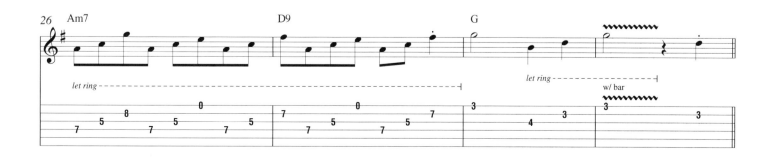

**D**

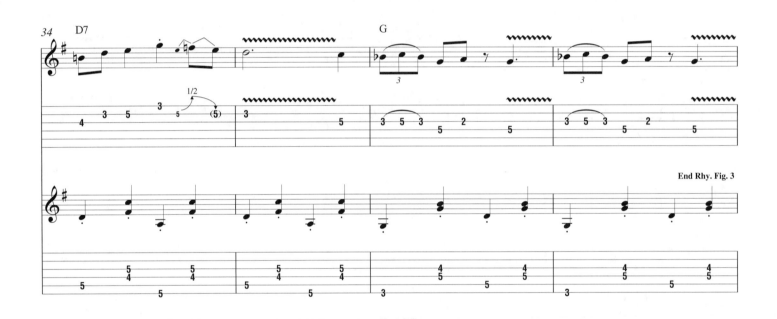

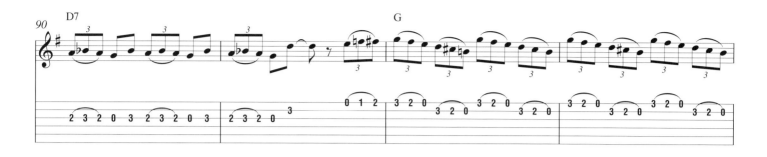

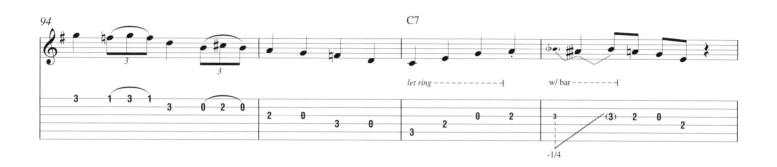

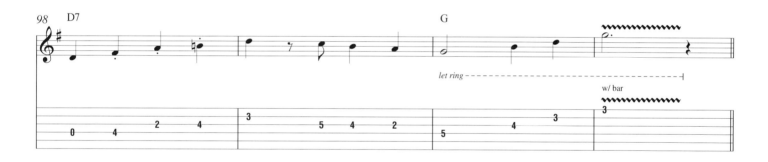

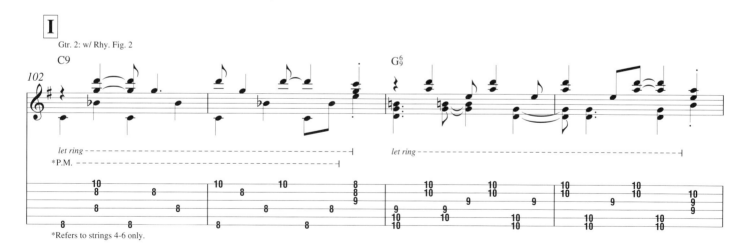

*Refers to strings 4-6 only.

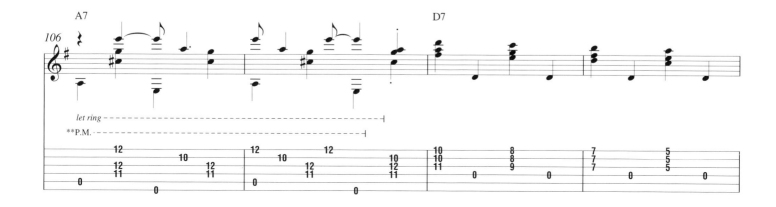

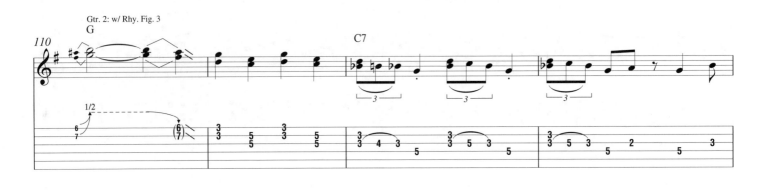

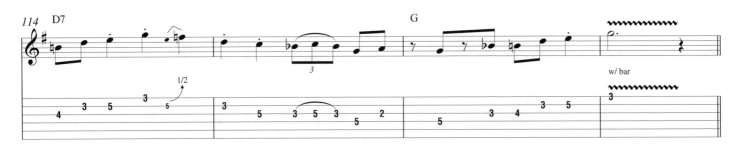

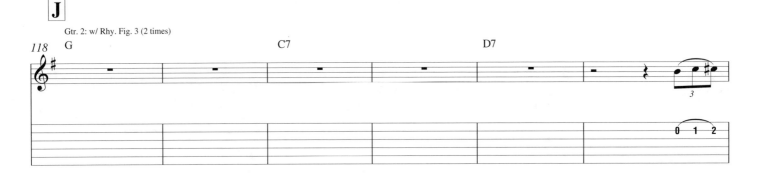

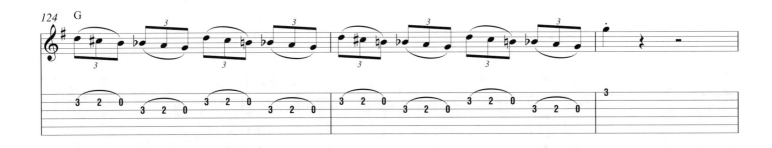

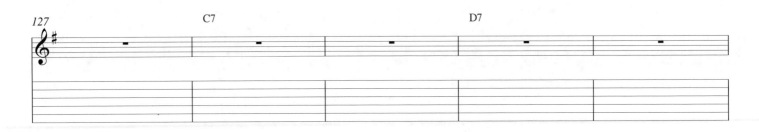

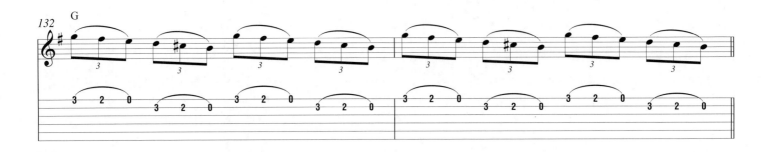

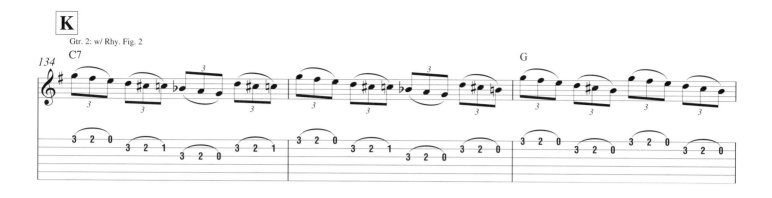

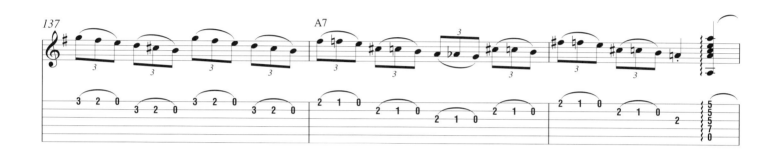

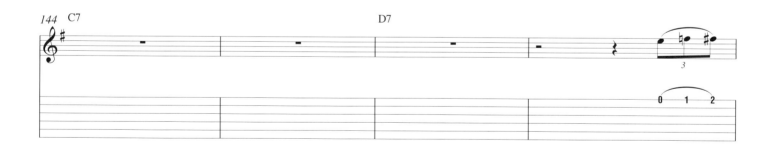

# Cannon Ball Rag
## (Me and Jerry, 1970)

Chet Atkins recorded and performed duets with a number of other ace guitarists over the years—from rock players like Mark Knopfler to rock/fusion/jazz players like Larry Carlton to acoustic fingerpickers like Tommy Emmanuel and Merle Travis to jazz legends like George Benson and Les Paul, and everything in between. But perhaps his best and most lively collaborations were with flashy country picker Jerry Reed. Not only do the two have a natural comfort about their playing together that translates into a "pickin' 'round the backyard" feel, but they also manage to coax each other into some pretty fiery performances; their chemistry on "Cannon Ball Rag" is no exception. Atkins released the track on his 1970 album, *Me and Jerry*—the first of three recordings by the duo—and it promptly went on to win a Grammy for Best Country Instrumental at the 1971 Grammy Awards. Jerry Reed released their second duet the following year, *Me and Chet*, which was also nominated for a Grammy but didn't win the award. Two decades later, the pair teamed up for their final duo recording, 1991's *Sneakin' Around*, which, unsurprisingly, *also* won a Grammy (another Best Country Instrumental at the 1993 Grammys). Atkins also paid tribute to his pal Jerry on a solo 1974 release, *Chet Atkins Picks on Jerry Reed*, where he recorded a full album of Jerry's material.

One of Atkins' heroes, Merle Travis, wrote "Cannon Ball Rag," and you can also find recordings and performances online of Atkins playing the tune with Travis, as well as with Travis's son, Thom Bresh.

In the song transcription on page 56, both Chet and Jerry's parts are shown, with Atkins' electric guitar shown on top and Reed's nylon-string acoustic shown on the bottom.

## Letter A

This section is a great study in rolls since *both* players play roll patterns throughout nearly the entire section! In the hands of less accomplished players, attempting to play roll patterns *together* might end up sounding like a wall of notes. But Atkins and Reed manage to blend their rolls together to create a thick-sounding harmonized roll. Aside from the fact that they're great pickers, several other things help contribute to this: they play 1) similar chord voicings, but play them on different parts of the neck, so that the notes don't get in the way of each other, and 2) they use *exactly the same* roll pattern with their picking hands.

First, let's take a look at the shapes they both play in measures 1–17. Chet's chord shapes are on the top, and Jerry's are on the bottom:

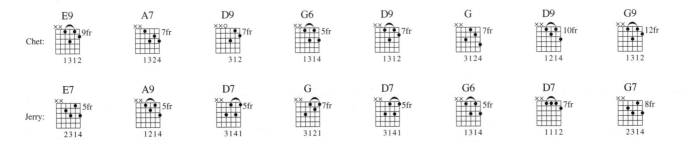

As you can see, both players play similar chord types, though occasionally they use slightly different embellishments. For instance, one person might play a sixth chord while the other plays a major chord, or one might play a seventh chord while the other plays a ninth. But these are simply colorful additions that fill out the sound more. Regardless of exactly the chord type, the most important thing is that they're playing different *inversions* of the chord (the notes are arranged in a different order, from low to high). For the most part, Atkins stays a few frets above Reed, but notice how he pops down for the fourth chord, where he plays a G6 several frets below Reed's G major shape. Playing inversions like this naturally creates some great harmonies, but you'll also find some interesting quirks that arise to spice things up a little. Let's take a closer look at how a few of these chords blend. If we look at the first set of chords (E9 and E7), putting the notes of both Chet's and Jerry's rolls together creates a roll harmonized in 3rds for *every note*! (Pretty amazing on guitar, where shapes aren't all uniform or identical):

But when we reach the third pair of chords—where Atkins plays a D9 against Reed's D7—we see a different story. Here, even though Chet's playing farther up the neck, he's playing that open D string, causing his part to overlap Jerry's part by starting out lower and then leaping up to higher notes. And when you put the notes together, you actually see that their shapes overlap a little—on the seventh fret. So on those notes, we see unison F♯ notes. Variations like that contrast extremely well with the perfectly harmonized 3rds in the E chords to help make the arrangement as a whole sound more interesting than if it was harmonized exactly the same way all the way through:

You'll note that in the previous examples, we didn't look at the tablature, because the interesting thing there was how the notes from each part blend with each other. Plus, trying to play both parts together is near impossible!

Aside from the shapes themselves, both Atkins and Reed play the exact same roll pattern throughout the first 17 measures—a common roll pattern and one of Atkins' favorites, as we've seen in previous tunes. Master this pattern, and you've pretty much mastered the section.

Cannon Ball Rag
Example 1

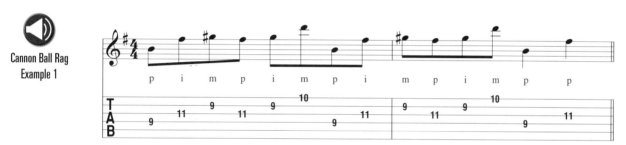

And one word about the final note of each roll pattern (beat 4 in the second measure): don't worry about it too much! The roll itself is a precise thing, with the thumb, index, and middle fingers plucking strings 4–2 in order, followed by the strings 3–1, and then repeated. But on that last note of the second measure, Atkins just brushes up with his thumb and hits whatever notes of the chord he happens to get. Look through and you'll see this is the case, as he hits the second and third strings in measure 2, the top two strings in measure 4, and just the third string in measure 6. The *only* place you really need to pay attention to this note is when he's using it as a chromatic passing tone to move from one chord to the next—basically any time he's *not* staying on the chord for that note (measures 8, 9, and 11). A *chromatic passing tone* moves by a half step—the distance of one fret—between two scale tones.

At measure 18, the duo plucks out a neat progression with quick-changing chords that shift every two beats (C–C♯°7–G7/D–E7/B–E♭7/B♭–D7/A–G). Chet's part is all written out with one set of stems, but he actually starts playing alternate bass at this point. Sometimes it helps to see the separation between thumb and fingers with split stems. Of course, since those inadvertent open strings picked by the fingers on the "and" of beats 2 and 4 overlap the bass notes, this would make it also look a little more confusing in some ways! But here you can easily see where the thumb plays to help you get into the alternate-bass mindset:

Cannon Ball Rag
Example 2

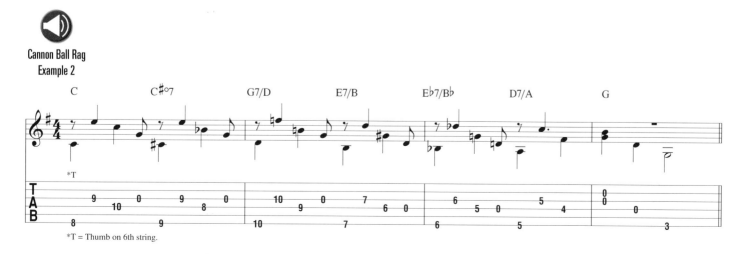

*T = Thumb on 6th string.

During those previously mentioned inadvertent open strings, Atkins is focused on changing chords. So, just like on that final note in the roll pattern section, don't worry too much about what string you're hitting there. You can see that as his fret-hand fingers move to grab the next chord, he's just playing an open string. It goes by so quickly that it doesn't really affect the sound, but it's a good idea to make sure not to accent these notes. They provide some extra momentum to the line, which is good. But playing them a little more quietly than the others will give you the best effect. In the final measure, Atkins just reaches up and plucks each note with a brush from his thumbpick.

While this book is about Chet, and not Jerry, it's interesting to note one small difference in the way they approached fingerpicking. While they both would use the thumb (or thumbpick) and three fingers, they each tended to favor the thumb and two fingers—just different ones! Chet would concoct incredibly complex picking patterns with just his thumb, index, and middle fingers. Jerry, on the other hand, would often tuck his index finger up into his hand and use just his middle and ring fingers along with the thumb. He apparently had arthritis in that index finger, and that's why he'd curl it under and favor his middle finger. Incidentally, this made his hand resemble a "claw," which is where the term came from that inspired him to name one of his tunes "The Claw." In this particular passage, however, Jerry probably unfurled that index finger and used all three fingers in conjunction with the thumb. The alternative would be to cross the fingers with the thumb on nearly every beat—certainly possible, but nowhere near as accurate of a way to go for this line:

**Cannon Ball Rag**
**Example 3**

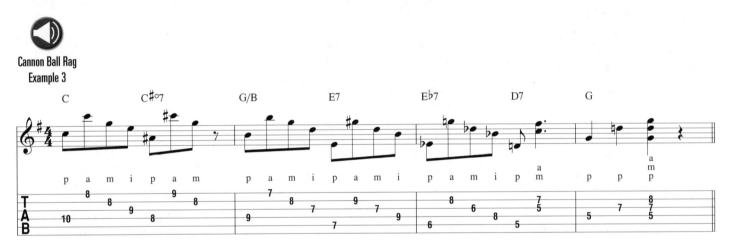

## Letter B

Letter A served as a long intro over the basic chord progression, so when we get to Letter B, we hit the ground running with the melody of the tune. Both players shift over to alternate-bass fingerpicking, but they keep the underlying philosophy from Letter A intact, where they each play chord shapes in different inversions to create a harmonized-sounding melody and bass simultaneously. Here, Atkins plays the melody, while Reed finds chord shapes that harmonize with the melody higher up the neck.

Throughout this section, Atkins alternates with his thumb on the lower strings and uses his index and middle fingers on the second and first strings, respectively:

**Cannon Ball Rag**
**Example 4**

As we've seen in previous songs, Atkins wraps his thumb over the neck to fret the bass notes of some of these chords (noted with a "T" between notation and tablature staves). For the first E7 chord, you'll recognize it as one of the E7 shapes that Jerry used in Letter A during the rolls. But here, Atkins alternates that low open E string with the thumb-fretted B note (the 5th), as shown in the following pictures:

When you reach the D9 chord in measure 26, don't worry about trying to thumb-fret the sixth *and* fifth strings with your thumb. While this is something Chet's likely to do, it's much more difficult than the alternative, which is what he fortunately does this time. What is that alternative?—rocking between the bottom two strings with your middle finger.

When Chet reaches the G chord in measure 28, he resumes his thumb fretting for the G chord instead of playing a full barre chord. Use your thumb on the sixth string and then place your ring, pinky, and middle fingers on the fifth, fourth, and third strings, respectively. Then barre with your index finger across the top two strings, for this shape:

G

T34211

Since Atkins alternates between the sixth and fourth strings in the bass (leaving out that fifth string), you *could* leave out that fifth string in your shape, which is easier to play and doesn't require the pinky:

G

T 3211

But, we'll use that string later, so you might as well get comfortable with the shape now! When you fret with your thumb like this, you have more fingers to move around and grab melody notes on top. But another benefit in this context is that your hand doesn't have to shift *down* the fretboard as much between the D9 and G chords. It's a subtle difference, but try alternating the D9 shape with a full G barre chord at the third fret, and you'll get the picture. If you thumb-fret the chord, the thumb slides down, and the index finger moves into place at the third fret without having to move your whole hand that much; your hand essentially pivots (or twists) around a point on the fretboard rather than *moving down* the fretboard completely. However, the full barre chord requires you to shift your whole hand down a little to get that index finger all the way up and over the complete fretboard.

After you follow the first ending to the repeat, head back to play the section once more. Once you reach the second ending, you'll have to slide your index finger up to get the D♯ note at the fourth fret.

## Letter C

At this point, Atkins continues on picking with the same technique as the previous section, while Reed goes back to the roll patterns from Letter A to give this section a contrasting sound. Atkins starts with a common seventh shape—the C7 shape slid up two frets—for his opening C7 chord. Here, the added ringing open high E string provides the 9th on top (E). Just like we did with the D9 chord in the previous section, we'll rock between the bottom two strings with one of our fingers—this time it's the ring finger.

Again, you'll have to slide that index finger up a fret to grab the D# note on the "and" of beat 3 in measure 32. When you reach the G6 chord in measure 33, use a similar shape to the thumb-fretted G chord in Letter B. But here, instead of barring those top two strings with your index finger, just fret the second string—letting that high E string ring open for the 6th of the chord (E). Here, Atkins alternates between all three of the bottom strings, so here's our payoff for using all of our fingers to fret this chord (see Letter B for a recap).

Atkins repeats the D9–G6 shapes again, then slaps his index finger across the top two string to cap it off in measure 38–creating that same full G shape we used in Letter B. Atkins and Reed then close out the section with the same quick-changing chord progression they used at the end of Letter A. They even pick it pretty much exactly the same way, though you'll note that Atkins may inadvertently pick a different open string right before each chord change.

## Letter D—Atkins Lead

At Letter D, Atkins jumps in for his lead section. While Reed switches back to an alternate-bass fingerpicking backdrop, Atkins begins with a new two-measure roll pattern on the top three strings. Here's the roll, which is a repeating m-i-p pattern. He repeats this pattern in exactly the same way for the A9 and D13 chords, so once you have it down here, you'll just need to fret the other chords and you're good to go:

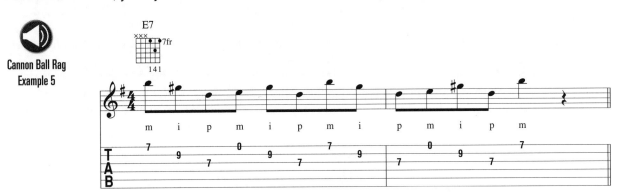

Cannon Ball Rag
Example 5

One very cool wrinkle about this line is that Atkins lifts his finger off of the first string for every other roll, alternating a fretted note up the neck (B) with the open high E string. One of his signature moves, whether it's with chord shapes or scalar runs, this adds an extra layer of sound to the line with that open string filling in a note between the other fretted strings. Check it out for yourself. First, try out the roll pattern with one static shape up the neck and then see how it sounds when you lift your finger off the high E string for every other roll:

Cannon Ball Rag
Example 6

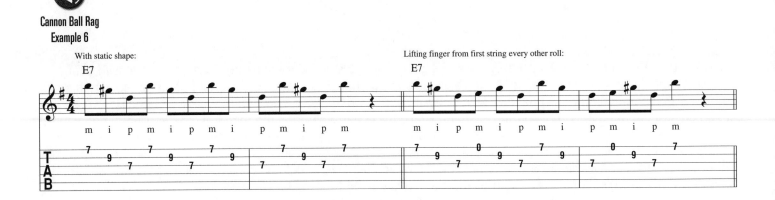

At measure 49, Atkins uses a descending G run similar to his oft-used triplet pull-off lines. Played as eighth notes, however, this one's slow enough for him to pick through most of the notes, alternating with his thumb and index finger, like this:

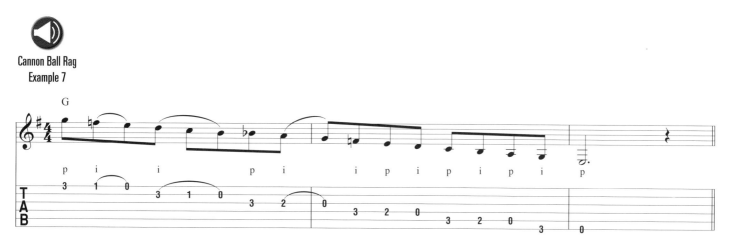

Cannon Ball Rag
Example 7

In measures 51–56, Atkins lays back and plays around with chord shapes by sliding into each one from a half step (one fret) above. This is a great trick to add to your bag, since it creates a lot of discord and release. Any time you play a chord one fret away from the underlying chord, you're creating a huge amount of tension because most every note will clash with that underlying chord. But when you slide back into the consonant sounding chord, all the tension is released. All Atkins does here is target chord shapes and inversions of the background chord, based on three-, four-, and even five-note shapes. Here are the shapes he's sliding around:

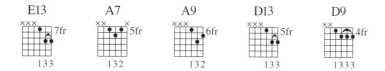

Once these shapes are under your fingers, you just have to move them up a fret, play them on the last beat of each measure, and then slide into the original shape one fret lower for the downbeat of the measure. Atkins plays around with the rhythm here a little, playing the pickup to the D13 chord in measure 55 on the "and" of beat 3 (instead of beat 4) and then sliding the pickup to the following D9 shape even further to beat 3. He finishes it off by just picking the top three strings of the shape.

In measures 57–58, he closes out this eight-bar section (measures 51–58) by resuming the roll pattern he played at the beginning of Letter D—this time over the top three strings of a G major chord at the third fret. Remember to lift your finger off the first string for every other roll!

Next, Atkins pulls off one the most difficult passages of the song by playing his signature cascading harmonics in measures 59–66. But with all the parentheses, slurs, and markings between tab and notation, part of the difficulty is getting over the intimidation of so much ink on the page! In actuality, Atkins' underlying thought process here is not nearly as intimidating as it looks. The finished technique is no picnic, but let's take a look at how he gets to the end result by gradually building up to it. The foundation of these licks was borne out of Atkins visualizing and playing just three drop-2 voicings on the top four strings:

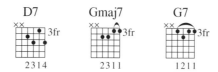

Next, let's look at how he's embellishing these chord shapes *without the harmonics*. Hold the complete chord shape with your fret hand as you go and play those pull-offs with your pinky finger. The pinky will, of course, have to move down to the second string for the pull-off there. Pluck the third and fourth strings with your thumb and the first and second strings with your ring (or middle) finger. This will leave your index finger free for the harmonics later. For the D7 shape, you'll need to barre that index finger across the third fret. That way, when you pull off from the fifth fret of the first string, you'll have something to pull off *to* (aside from the open strings)!

Cannon Ball Rag
Example 8

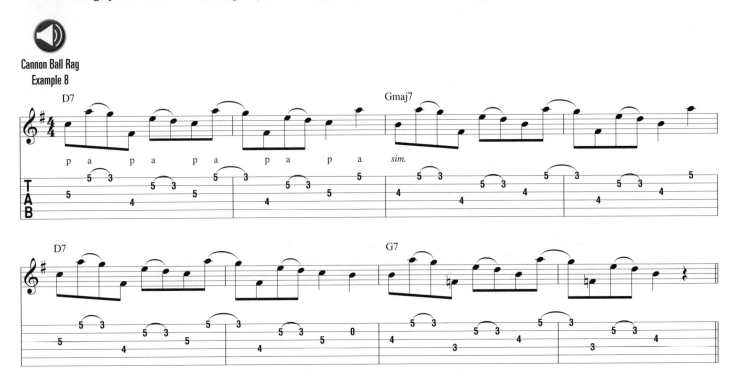

As you can see, this part is fairly straightforward (relatively speaking). It even falls nicely under the pick-hand fingers, since we're alternating between the thumb and ring (or middle) finger for every pluck. The tricky thing here is that those pull-offs on the top two strings add an extra eighth note into the mix, which throws our picking into syncopated territory—instead of playing a full cycle of thumb/middle every beat, we're doing it every 1-1/2 beats.

Next, let's just try out the harmonics on their own. Keep your fretting hand in place holding down the full chord shapes. Then, touch the string 12 frets higher with your pick-hand's index finger and pluck behind it (closer to the bridge) with your thumb.

Work on this until you have those harmonics ringing out clearly throughout.

Cannon Ball Rag
Example 9

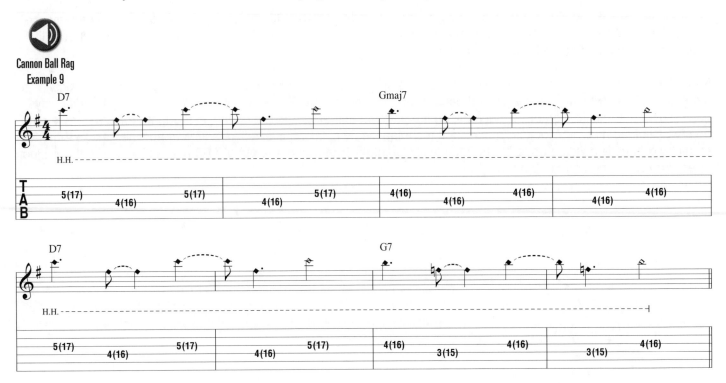

Once you have that down, add the other notes back in and—voila—you're playing the finished set of cascading harmonic licks!

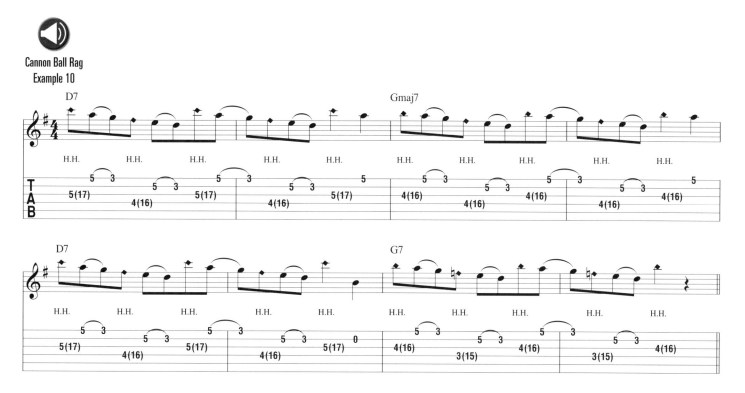

Cannon Ball Rag
Example 10

Atkins continues with artificial harmonics for the final four measures of his break but adds another twist as he starts plucking double stops instead of single notes. Here, he turns a simple sliding-6th move into a difficult one by playing the artificial harmonics on the bottom note while simultaneously plucking a regular note on top. Because that lower note sounds an octave higher when played as an artificial harmonic, this turns those 6ths into chiming 3rds.

For measures 67–68, slide your fret-hand's middle and ring fingers up the fretboard to grab the notes on the third and first strings, respectively. The tricky part here is the picking, but it's similar to the previous section. This time, though, you'll touch the third string 12 frets above the fretted note and pluck that string while also plucking the first string with your ring (or middle) finger.

As you reach the slide in measure 68, pluck the grace note double stop at the sixth fret (touching the string at the 18th fret with your index finger) and, after the notes sound, simply slide your fret-hand fingers up a fret to the seventh fret. You don't need to re-sound the harmonic here. Once you pluck it at the 6th/18th-fret combination, the harmonic will *sound* as if it's sliding up a half step, even though you're not playing it again. The same thing holds true for the quarter-tone bend heading into the next measure. Play the double stop (with harmonic) and bend the strings with your fret-hand fingers down at the fifth fret; the harmonic note will bend up, as well.

In the second half of measure 69, Atkins continues to play double stops, but here he's not *thinking* in double-stop shapes, like he was in the previous measures. Instead, he frets this G6 chord in anticipation of the resolution to G in measure 70:

G6

Then, with his picking hand, he outlines the chord shape by plucking pairs on strings 1 and 3 and then moves down to strings 2 and 4. (Remember that you'll have to move that index finger between the 16th and 17th frets to highlight the shape of the chord 12 frets higher.) Outlining chord shapes like this to play harmonics was one of Atkins' brilliant tricks, which he'd occasionally use to create both the cascading harmonic runs of the previous section or the double-stop or chordal type harmonic sounds of this G6 chord.

## Letter E—Reed Lead

At Letter E, Atkins takes a back seat while Reed jumps to the forefront for his lead section. Here, Chet holds down chord shapes and simply alternates between the bass note and higher strings with his thumb for nearly the entire section.

While we're focusing on Atkins' playing for this book, let's just take a quick moment to notice how Reed creates some very cool and interesting sounding licks by operating out of chord positions around the fretboard and mixing those with open strings. Throughout measures 71–94, he pretty much anchors his hand in a chord-shape position for each chord, accessing notes around those shapes and mixing them with open strings. (The one partial exception is the G chord, where he's moving from the shape shown here to a bunch of open-string licks at the nut.) Line these chord shapes up with each two-measure section to compare the shapes and the licks he plays in each.

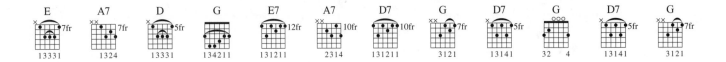

In measures 95–98, the chords start moving by so quickly that it's tough to play licks around the shapes. Perhaps because of this, Reed targets a fun lick that plays off the ♭3rd and major 3rd of the G chord in measure 96. At this point, he's operating around the C-shape version of the G chord up at the seventh fret, though this is one of those nifty licks that's permanently ingrained in his fingers, wherever he plays it:

Cannon Ball Rag
Example 11

The nifty move he pulls off here, though, actually happens *before* this lick. Check out how he creates a little tension by sliding this lick *down* a half step in the previous measure, moving up into the G lick for a resolution. In measure 97, he manages to keep up with the chord progression by accessing licks around the following two shapes:

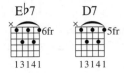

And by measure 98, he ties up his break with some G6 and G chords.

## Coda

After Chet and Jerry take their lead breaks, they head back to the beginning to reprise the intro section as an outro. After they finish this section, they head to the coda, where each takes a two-bar break to finish off the piece. First up is Reed, who again plays some crafty licks out of these two chord positions, playing off that bluegrass-inspired interplay between the ♭3rd and major 3rd of G:

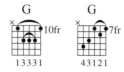

Chet finishes off the tune with another nice cascading harmonic—this time with all natural harmonics alternating between the between the 12th and seventh frets for the ascending harmonics, and finishing off with one harmonic at the fifth fret, like this:

Cannon Ball Rag
Example 12

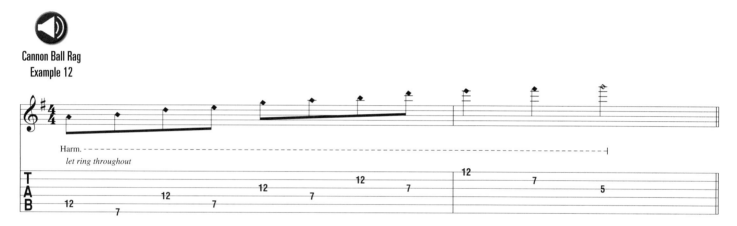

Cannon Ball Rag
Full Song   **A**

# CANNON BALL RAG
By Merle Travis

Moderately fast ♩ = 138

*Chord symbols reflect combined harmony.

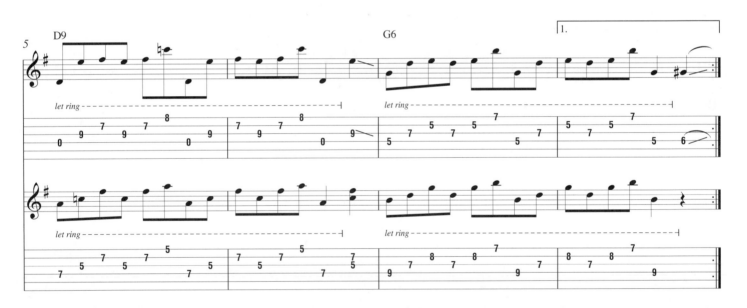

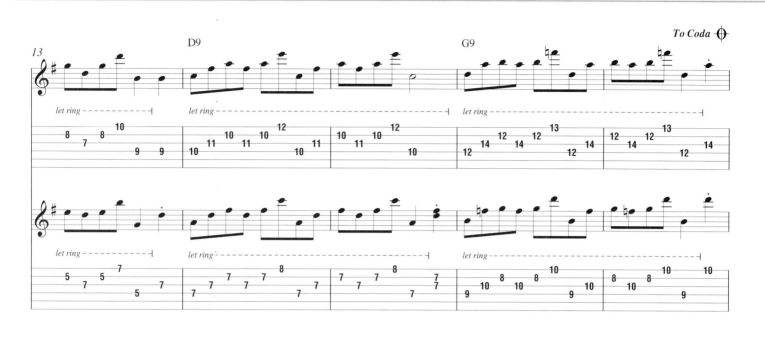

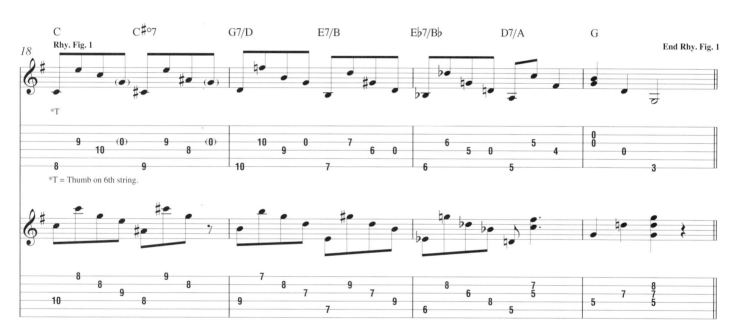

*P.M. on downstemmed notes only.

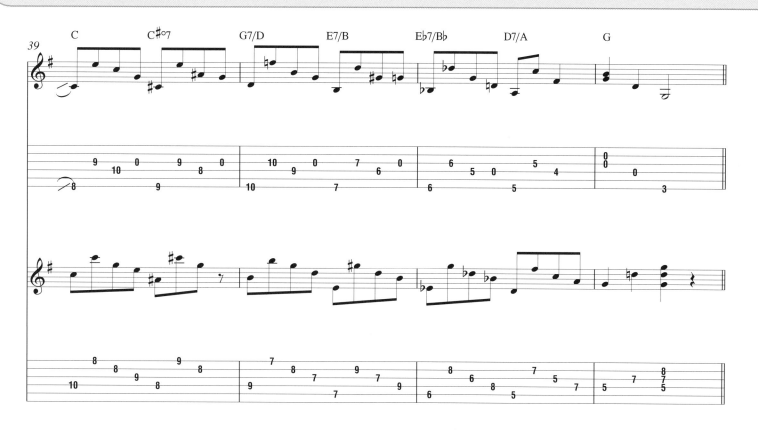

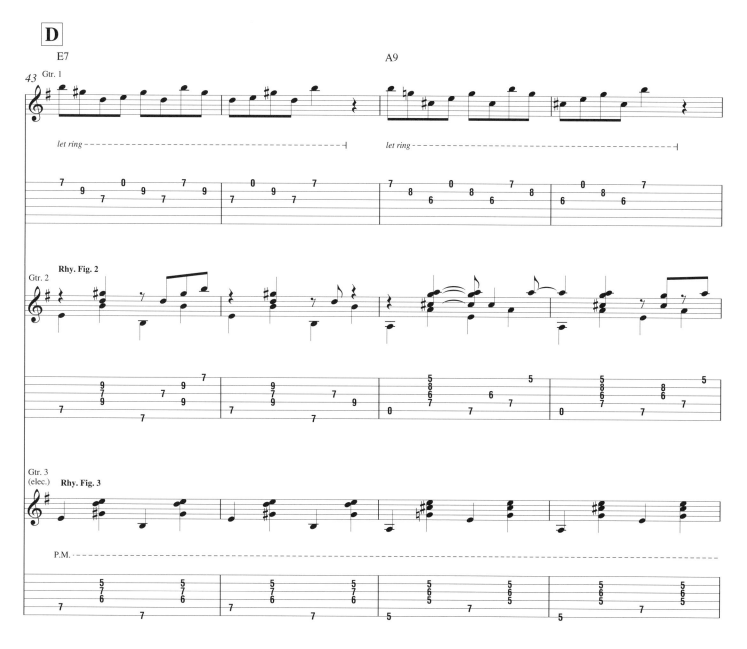

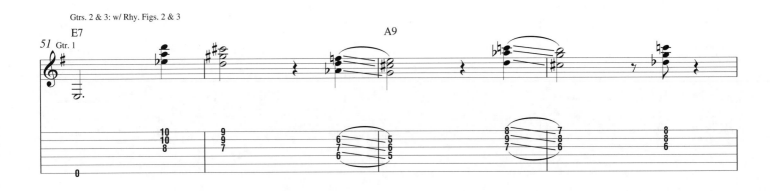

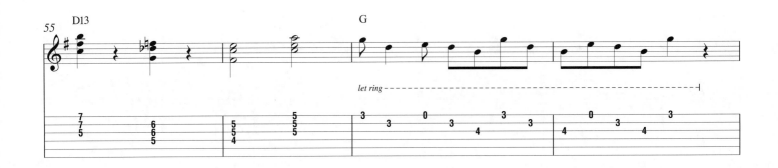

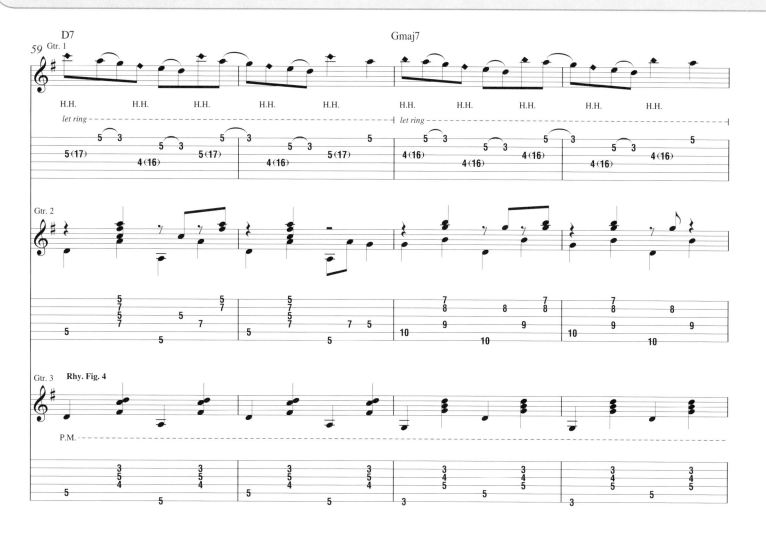

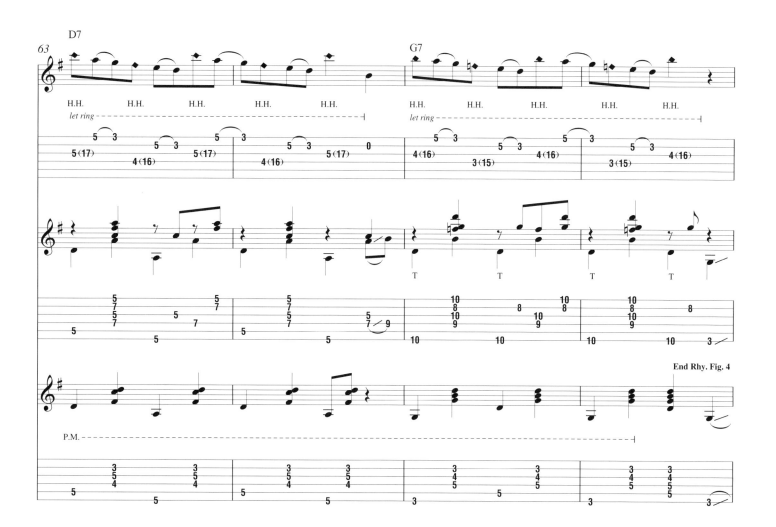

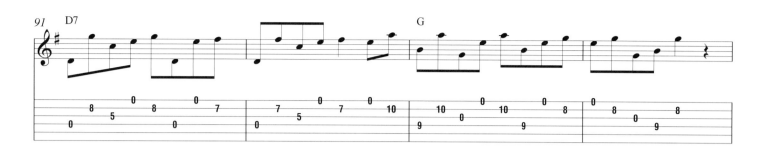

*D.S. al Coda*
*(take repeat)*

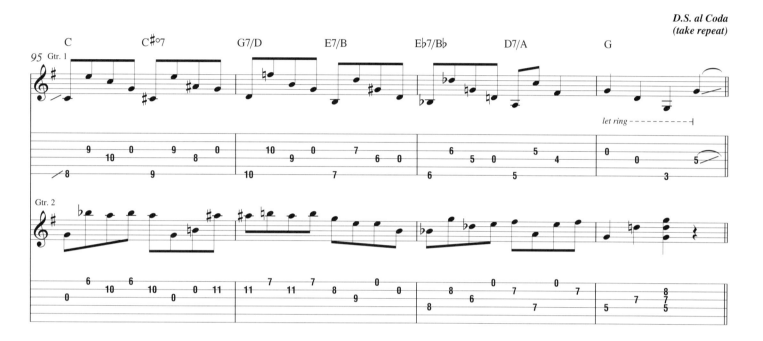

**Coda**

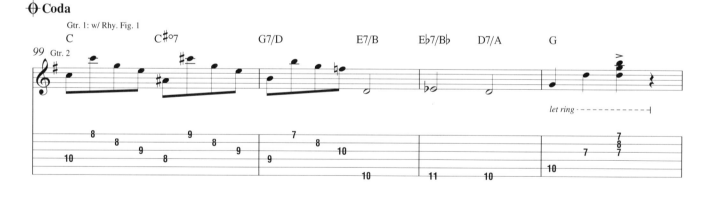

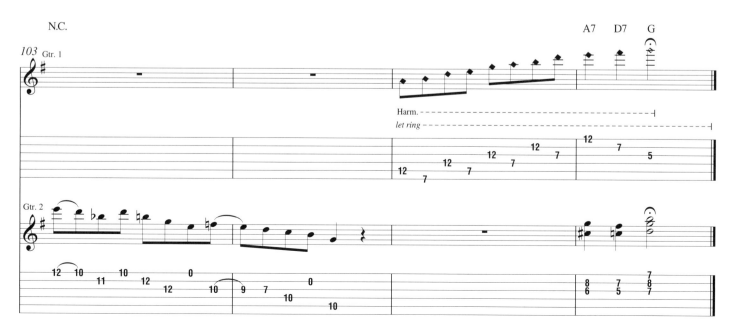

# The Entertainer
## (*Chet Atkins Goes to the Movies*, 1976)

Chet Atkins earned a Grammy for his performance of "The Entertainer" in 1976. Included on his then-current release, *Chet Atkins Goes to the Movies*, the tale of the record and how it came to be is also a story about Atkins and his friendship with and support of other guitarists. Atkins reportedly met guitarist and teacher John Knowles at a rehearsal for the Dallas Symphony Orchestra, and Knowles later mailed Atkins his arrangement of Scott Joplin's classic ragtime piano song, "The Entertainer." Atkins liked the tune enough that he recorded it, and Knowles later got a call from Jim Crockett, the editor of *Guitar Player* magazine, who'd heard about the recording. Crockett wanted Knowles to ask Atkins about recording a complete record of movie arrangements, and he wanted *Guitar Player* to publish a book of the songs, which Knowles would transcribe. With a simple phone call, the project came to fruition, Knowles added three more of his own arrangements, and the book was published (including nine of the songs from the record). Knowles and Atkins developed a long-standing friendship, and Atkins even bestowed his C.G.P. award (Certified Guitar Player) on Knowles in 1996. Incidentally, another great guitarist (and friend of Chet's) who was given the C.G.P. designation also contributed an arrangement to the record: Lenny Breau.

## Letter A

Before you get started, make sure to tune your sixth string down to D, bringing your guitar into drop D tuning, as Chet did for the song. "The Entertainer" is played slowly enough that you can pick the single-note intro several ways. One way you could do this would be to use your thumb only and pick all downstrokes. Another way would be to hold your index finger and thumb together, using the thumbpick as you would a pick held between your index finger and thumb (or by using your thumbnail, if you're not playing with a thumbpick). Try the pattern shown below for one of the easier ways to pick through these opening measures using this technique (which is similar to how Chet did it):

The Entertainer
Example 1

Alternatively, you could use your middle or ring finger for all of the upstrokes in the previous example, leaving your thumb to play those downstrokes. But there are many ways that would work here, so experiment with it if none of these are comfortable for you.

For the fretting hand, try out the fingerings shown in the previous example to get you through this section. The first measure doesn't pose much of a problem; all you need to do here is slightly shift to a lower position by bringing your ring finger down to the 12th fret of the second string and letting your other fingers move down to grab the notes at the ninth and 10th frets. But the second measure has two seventh-fret notes in a row. While many rock or jazz players might roll across the strings to fret both of these notes with the same finger, Atkins opts for more of the classical approach, fretting each note with a different finger. Again, this naturally shifts your hand down a fret as you use the middle finger—instead of the index finger—to fret the D note on the seventh fret of the third string, which gives you easy access to the sixth-fret C♯ note with your index finger.

The "rit." marking between notation and tablature staves stands for *ritardando* (also often shortened to "ritard."), and it simply means to slow down. So, in the middle of the third measure, start gradually slowing down as you head into the last measure of the intro section.

## Letters B–C

At Letter B, Atkins begins his alternate-bass accompaniment. Note that in the transcription, the stems are split between melody parts (upstems) and bass parts (downstems)—not between parts that the fingers play and that the thumb plays (which is sometimes the case). This helps you see which parts should be brought to the forefront and held out as the melody and which parts are supposed to be the accompaniment. But it does make it harder to know which notes you need to play with the thumb. Generally speaking, everything with stems pointing down should be played with your thumb, and a "p" marking has been added between notation and tablature for every upstemmed note that you should play with your thumb, as well. There are some exceptions to this. In measure 12, for example, all the notes on beat 2 are stemmed down, even though Chet plays these with his thumb, index, and middle. This is done because the melody note is the high open E string in this case, and it needs to ring out for two full beats. Or in measure 6 on beat 2, Chet plays the open D and G strings with his thumb and index, respectively, even though they're both stemmed down. So another general rule to keep in mind might be this: When there is more than one note stemmed down, play the lowest with your thumb.

But the even trickier thing that happens here is the careful integration of thumb and fingers to play melody and accompaniment—or, more specifically, using your thumb to play both "background" bass notes and "foreground" melody notes—which requires quite a bit of dynamic control over your thumb and fingers. For example, take a look at the first four measures:

The Entertainer
Example 2

Drop D tuning: (low to high) D-A-D-G-B-E

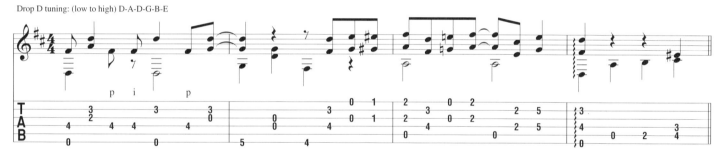

In the first two measures (measures 5–6 in the transcription), Atkins plays pretty much strict alternate bass with his thumb, adding melody on top. But check out beat 2 of the first measure, where he plays a bass note on the fourth string with his thumb and follows that immediately with a melody note using his index finger. Here, you have to make sure the note you pluck with your thumb is loud enough to hear and provide forward rhythmic momentum, but it also has to be quiet enough that it doesn't take away from the melody, because the very next instant you need to pluck that note with your finger and make it loud enough to carry through as a melody note. It's a subtle point, but it's incredibly important in bringing an arrangement to life; otherwise, you won't hear a distinct melody at all—just a bunch of notes!

But then, Atkins comes back on beat 4 and plays that melody note with his thumb! This makes perfect sense, since the thumb is already playing an alternate-bass pattern, so it's natural for the thumb to play that note. However, here you're playing the melody, so you need to bring that particular note out (instead of holding back, as you did earlier in the measure).

At the end of the second measure (measure 6 in the transcription), Atkins breaks out of alternate-bass fingerpicking and lets his fingers take care of the run of 6th intervals. Here, the thumb just plays steadily on beats 1 and 3 in measure 3.

This morphing in and out of alternate-bass fingerpicking takes some getting used to, and it's the independence here that hints at what would eventually lead into the intricate style of modern fingerstyle guitar, where melody and accompaniment rely on no set patterns (though they may be integrated in and out). In Atkins' earlier electric recordings, he often moved in and out of alternate-bass playing, but when he moved out of it, he often went to more of a lead style that needed band backup—whether that was jumping into roll patterns, playing licks, scalar runs, or short chord-melody snippets. Here, he continues to provide accompaniment as he breaks away from the alternate bass.

As you play through, don't forget that you're in drop D tuning! Since this moves the low E string down a whole step, that means you'll have to adjust your chord shapes by fretting that low bass note up two frets. In this four-measure passage, that means it will change these two shapes:

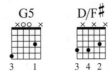

Note how Atkins frets that D/F♯ chord with his ring, pinky, and middle fingers, low to high. This allows his index finger to quickly get over for the E♯/G♯ double stop on the "and" of beat 4, which he plays by barring across the first fret with his index finger. Then, slide that index-finger barre up one fret for the D/A chord on beat 1 of the next measure, reaching down for the D/F♯ dyad with your middle and ring fingers. Use that index-finger barre again for the dyads on the second fret (the "and" of beats 2 and 3) and reach over with your pinky and ring finger for the E/G dyad at the fifth fret. Also make sure to roll your pick-hand fingers on the D chord in the following measure, quickly picking in ascending order: thumb, index, middle (notated by the squiggly line to the left of the notes and tablature).

The "a tempo" marking between notation and tablature indicates that you should resume the original tempo. In the first four measures, the "rit." marking told us to slow down, and now this marking negates that, bringing us back up to the performance pace. The first time through, the melody (from Letter B to Letter C) slows down and speeds up quite a bit. It's a nice way to start the tune in dramatic fashion. Follow the "rit." and "a tempo" markings to perform it the way Atkins does, but you can always add your own tempo fluctuations based on what you feel sounds best. It's a great way to instill your own stamp on a tune.

Moving on to the next four measures, Atkins ends up providing alternate bass throughout this whole section. While this is easier to get the hang of, watch out for the end of that second measure (measure 10), because this is where the thumb dropped out in the previous four measures. However, here it keeps on chugging along, reaching up to pluck the bottom note of that set of three upstemmed notes. Roll your picking hand here again, quickly moving from thumb to index to middle. Then, in the next two measures, continue on with the thumb playing alternate bass while the fingers provide the melody.

Our drop D tuning affects one more chord shape in this phrase—the E9 chord:

Because we have to fret the sixth string, all four of our fingers are used up, and we don't have any left for the fifth string. But that doesn't really matter here, since we're fingerpicking the notes instead of strumming through whole chord shapes. As you can see, we never actually play that string. But to keep it from ringing through, roll your middle finger down till it touches the fifth string and dampens it so that it doesn't inadvertently sound.

Measures 13–16 are nearly identical to measures 5–8, except for the final measure, where the bass walks down, and the melody notes lead up into the next line. Measures 17–19 use a repeating melody on the top strings with the fingers while the thumb plays an alternate-bass pattern that walks down chromatically from D all the way to A. This series of chords is a common pattern in pop and rock, and the shapes are often fingered like this:

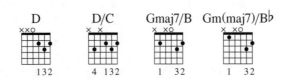

This may feel right to you and, if so, great! But, Atkins actually added a little twist by using his *middle* finger to play the bass note of the D/C chord. This creates a problem for fingering the high F♯ note of the D chord, though, but it's not too difficult if you follow Chet's lead. After the open first-string melody note on beat 2 of measure 17, flatten your index finger to barre across the top three strings, allowing you to grab the melody and harmony notes on the top two strings on the "and" of beat 2.

The previous melody/harmony notes you just played give your middle finger just a split second longer to get down to that bass note so it's ready and in place when you need to pluck it on beat 3.

For that open E melody note on beat 4, all you have to do now is roll your index finger out of the barre.

Try out Chet's way and use whichever way's the most comfortable for you. In measure 19, he adds a lower harmony a 6th interval below the melody line, using his index and middle fingers to pluck out each string pair. This, along with the following measure (measure 20), is actually identical to what you already played in measures 7–8.

Listen closely to the original recording and you'll hear the melody sound a little brighter here in measures 17–18, moving back to a less bright sound in measure 19. To achieve this brighter sound, move your picking hand closer to the bridge of the guitar. Experiment a bit with this and you'll see that the closer you get to the bridge, the brighter and sharper the tone sounds; the farther away from the bridge you pick, the darker and mellower it sounds.

Letter C essentially repeats the same melody and accompaniment from Letter B, but here Chet does away with the dramatic pauses (shown by the "rit." and "a tempo" markings) and plays straight through at a solid clip.

## Letter D

At Letter D, Atkins goes up the fretboard, and his thumb starts working double duty. For all of the harmonized melody in measures 37–38, his thumb plays the lowest note of the harmony—all on the fourth string (upstemmed notes). But his thumb *also* still plays those bass notes, which are played in the gaps between harmonized melody notes. This means that the thumb is playing for *every* eighth-note subdivision, whereas it only plays for each quarter-note subdivision throughout pretty much all of the rest of the piece. Let's hone in on those two measures, start slowly, and gradually work up as you get comfortable with the double thumb. Pick-hand fingerings are written in for both the upstemmed and downstemmed notes so that you can easily see how often your thumb needs to play. Use your middle and index fingers on the first and second strings, respectively.

The Entertainer
Example 3

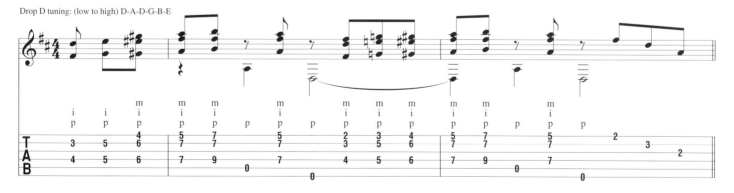

The fretting hand gets a bit of a workout here, too, since you need to slide three-note shapes around the fretboard for each eighth note. Follow the fingerings in the previous example to see exactly where to put each finger. Essentially, your ring finger frets everything on the fourth string, and your index finger frets everything on the first string. For the second string, you'll use either your pinky, middle, or index finger, depending on what note is being played. But there are really only these three shapes with which to familiarize yourself:

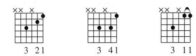

Looking at the several measures where we play these shapes, we can see that we only play the first shape once, play the second shape *three times* as we slide up the fretboard, and use the third shape once at the highest position, before sliding back to the second shape. Atkins would quickly move his index finger in and out of place for the barre across the top two strings in the third shape. If you have trouble flattening and raising that finger so quickly, you could try barring the top two strings with the index finger for all three shapes. This way, your finger will be right in place for the third shape when it arrives, and the barre won't affect the other shapes, since there are notes fretted by other fingers in front of it. But try both ways and use whichever way you find most comfortable.

In measure 39, Atkins returns to alternate-bass picking with his thumb while his fingers pluck the melody and harmony out on the top three strings. But he quickly dispenses with this again in the next measure (measure 40), as the thumb has to play two eighth notes quickly in a row to open the measure—the bass note on beat 1 and the F♯ melody note on the "and" of beat 1. This is another place where you'll need to focus closely on dynamics, because you want that bass note (played with the thumb) to be quieter than the melody note above, but then you'll need to play the *next* note with your thumb louder, to make it sound as though it's part of the melody. In fact, this is the start of a lower counter-melody line that's actually accented a little to bring it out, so you'll need to play that F♯ note even a little *louder* than the previous melody note. On beat 4, Atkins begins double-thumb duty again as he repeats the same line from the beginning of the section. This time, however, he continues up the fretboard at the end of measure 42 to play the higher melody notes, while resuming alternate-bass fingerpicking again underneath. But watch for that other quick double-thumb at the beginning of measure 44!

Here, he's operating out of full and partial chord shapes up the neck (all the way through measure 46) and accessing any melody notes that don't fall within these shapes by fretting those notes wherever they fall nearest each shape. As you can see, the A6, A7, and D shapes are all full four-string shapes, while the E6 shape he uses is a partial shape of an E6 barre chord based on an A-shape major barre chord.

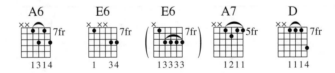

In the second half of this section (starting at measure 45), Atkins repeats the beginning of the first-half melody, but now we're playing it over an alternate-bass pattern with the thumb. Here, we start operating out of the D shape we just looked at before heading back towards the nut for the G chord in measure 47. He keeps playing alternate bass for these three full measures, but watch again for the quick double-thumb at the beginning of measure 48. The rest of the measure acts as a bit of a break, with his fingers picking everything. He closes the section out by resuming alternate-bass picking for measures 49–52. After following the D.S. marking to a reprise of Letter B, we head to the coda, which wraps things up nearly identically to the way Letter B closes. Here, however, we don't play a bass note on beat 1 of the final measure, prolonging the complete resolution to beat 3, where we use the top two notes of the same D shape we just looked at in Letter D. To match Atkins' feel on the record, make sure to follow the "rit." marking in these final two measures and gradually slow down as you approach the final chord.

The Entertainer
Full Song

# THE ENTERTAINER
### By Scott Joplin
### Arranged by John Knowles

Drop D tuning:
(low to high) D-A-D-G-B-E

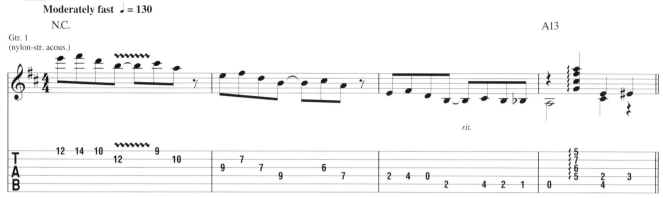

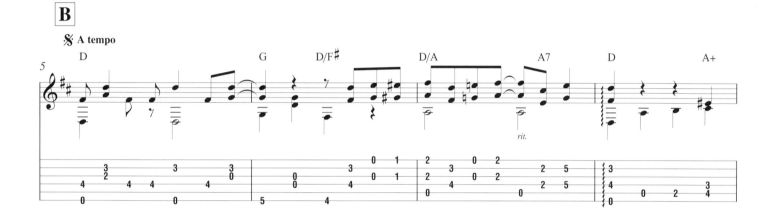

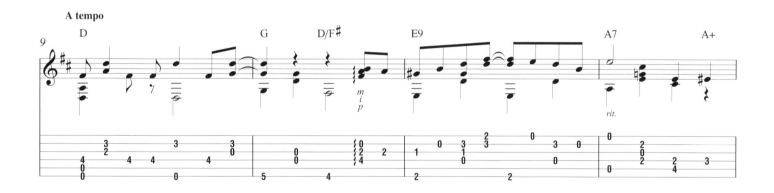

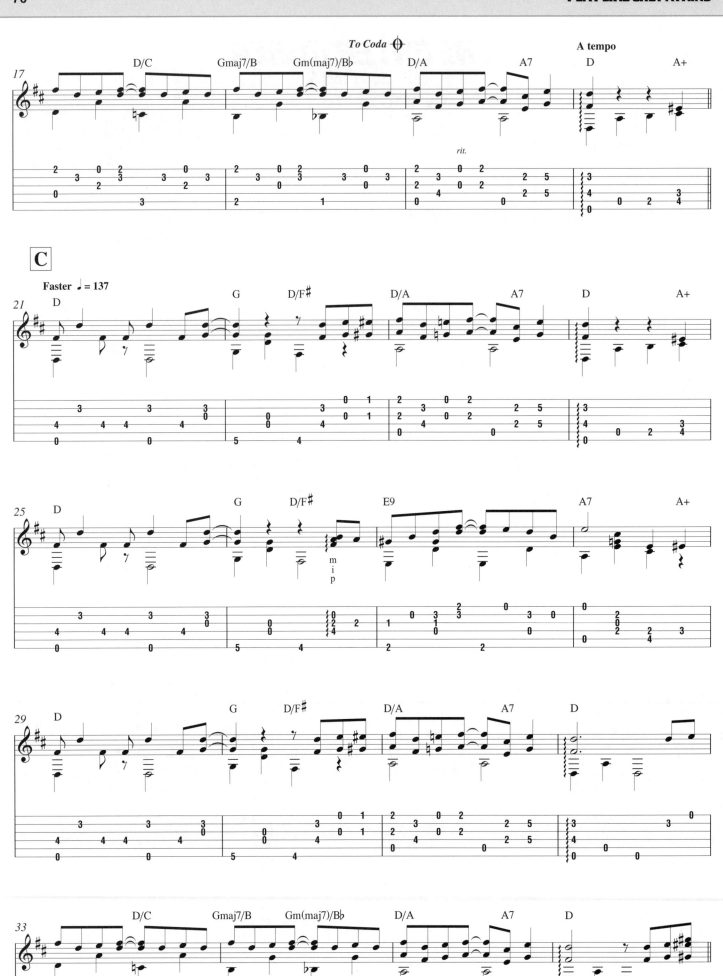

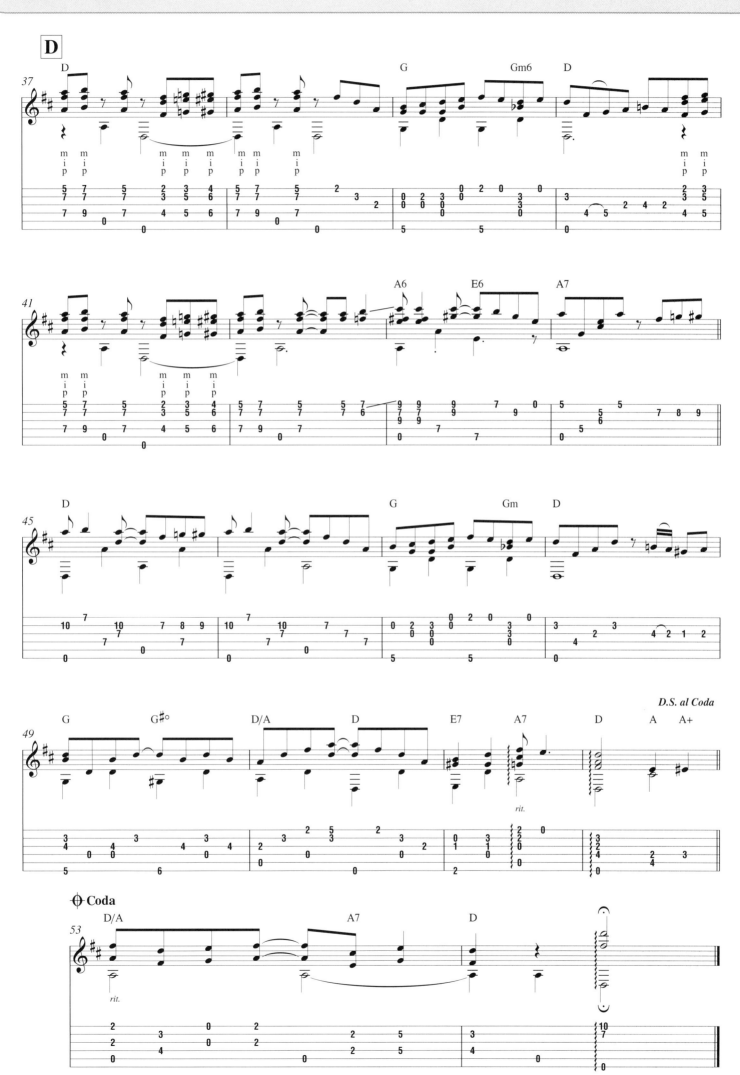

# ESSENTIAL LICKS

Many guitarists learn and create licks in conjunction with scale patterns on their guitar, whether they're playing a minor-pentatonic lick in a blues context, a major-scale based lick in rock, or a highly altered scale in jazz. And while Atkins certainly had integrated this approach into his bag of tricks, much of his playing was informed by the *way* he played the guitar—especially in reference to his picking hand. So, many of the essential licks in this section are grouped together based around the particular technique he used to coax them out of his guitar.

## Open-String Licks

When guitarists hear "open string" and "licks" together, they might think about licks down at the nut of the guitar, where the open strings are accessible alongside their fretted counterparts. Chet certainly played licks like these, but he was also a master at combining open strings with notes up the neck to create a multitude of different types of licks—which makes this one of the meatier sections.

### Scalar Licks up the Neck with Open Strings

Chet mixed notes up the neck with open strings to create a variety of great scalar-type licks (licks based around or sounding like a scale). When you fret notes up the neck like this, you can play closer intervals to the open strings below. This allows you to let the notes ring together more than you would if you were playing along adjacent strings, resulting in a ringing cascade effect.

### Lick 1

Here's how Atkins might play a G minor lick using this technique. If you look at the notes, this simply climbs up and down the G minor scale, but when you play it like this, it works much better as a lick than if you simply play the scale using two or three notes per string.

Follow the pick-hand markings between the notation and tablature for the most efficient way to pick this lick. It's a little quirky because you play just the thumb and index finger for the first two notes, then roll through the thumb, index, and middle fingers twice, and repeat the whole thing in reverse. But when you're applying this technique to a scale or idea, your fingers have to adapt to where the notes are on the fretboard, and that's all based on where the open strings are.

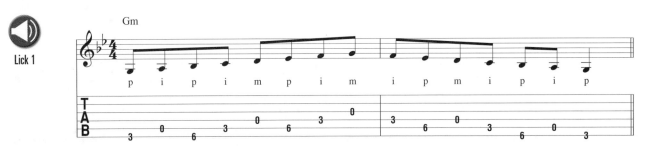

### Lick 2

Now, while you can use complete scales as licks with this method, you can apply these scales and patterns in many ways, as Atkins often did. Here's a Chet-style lick that employs the same concept, but we're not strictly playing a scale. Again, pay attention to those pick-hand markings. This one actually starts exactly the same way as the previous one: with a thumb-index combo before falling into a three-note thumb-index-middle pattern. A little tension is added to this lick by operating out of the C minor scale (with that E♭ note), even though Chet would typically play a lick like this in C major.

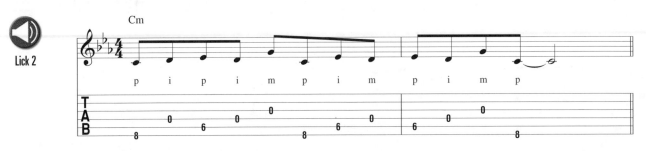

### Lick 3

Atkins also created licks that added an extra note or two to a scale, which likely happened based on where the notes fell on the strings (and may have even been a "happy accident" he encountered by applying a fingering across strings as he came up with a lick). Here's a typical example of this where we ascend a C major scale but pass through the ♭7th tone, B♭ (the same note as A♯, or its *enharmonic equivalent*). Check out here how we start the scale below the root, on the A note on the open fifth string. That ♭7th tone (the A♯) is conveniently located at the third fret as well. Once we reach the highest strings, we finish the lick by moving up the fretboard to resolve on the C note up at the eighth fret.

To play the cascading part of the lick in the first two measures, Atkins would use a thumb-index-middle (p-i-m) roll pattern, moving that pattern up each string set until he reaches the top string. Notice that a little wrinkle is added to the lick because you have to *start* by plucking the fifth string with the index finger before beginning the first roll down on the sixth string with the thumb.

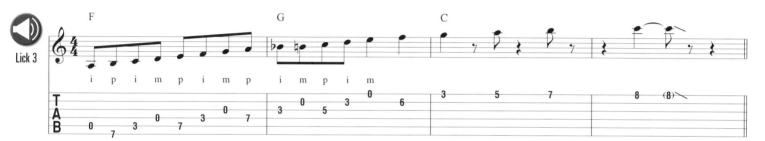

### Lick 4

Here's a similar idea that uses exactly the same pattern as the previous lick, except here we're playing it even more up to "Chet" tempo using 16th-note triplets. This one also ascends *and* descends, using the p-i-m pattern in reverse to get back down (m-i-p). When you reach the top string, your middle finger acts as a pivot between patterns, functioning as both the last note of the final ascending p-i-m pattern and the first note of the initial descending m-i-p pattern.

While the previous lick was played in the context of C major, Atkins would likely use this one in its relative minor key: A minor.

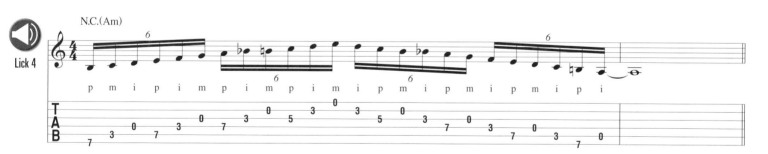

## Pull-Off Licks to Open Strings at the Nut

Chet was quite fond of these types of licks, which are based around three-note groups usually down near the nut of the guitar. He'd pull off in quick succession from the highest fretted note to the next one and then to the open string, often then repeating this pattern on other strings—sometimes using the same fingers/fret patterns, and sometimes varying his note/finger choices to highlight the background chords.

### Lick 5

Atkins often started these licks by playing a hammer-on figure leading up to the first pull-off combination. The following lick does this on the high E string before starting the pull-off from the third and second frets, using the ring and middle finger. The lick then descends through the second, third, and fourth strings using the same fingering pattern before landing on the low root G note on the sixth string. While we're in the key of G major, and the lick uses *mostly* the G major scale, notice the bluesy added ♭5th (C♯) and ♭3rd (B♭) that naturally fall into the lick when you use the same fingering/fret pattern across all strings.

Atkins played this lick in a 1957 TV performance of "Mister Sandman," which can be found online (the lick doesn't appear in his recorded version which is featured in the earlier transcription in this book).

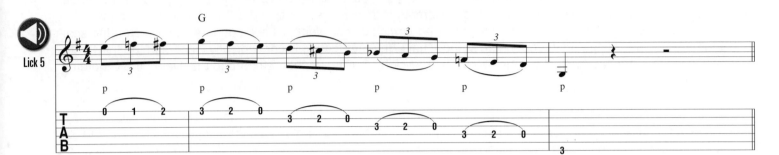

This type of lick is featured prominently in other parts of the book. For more examples, see Letter A, Letter K, and the closing bars of "Dizzy Strings" (in the "Songs" section), along with the "Black Mountain Rag" excerpt (in the "Signature Phrases" section).

## Pull-Off Licks to Open Strings up the Neck

This may sound an awful lot like the previous lick section, but that's not the case at all. The previous section focused on licks that pulled off in succession to the open strings in patterns that are repeated up and down the strings—usually in triplets. But when Atkins gets further up the neck, he's more likely to change things up rhythmically, rely less on a set single pattern, or pull off the same number of notes each time.

### Lick 6

In this one we operate out of fifth position, pulling off to the fifth fret (from the eighth or seventh fret) and then pulling off to the open string below. There actually is a pattern for this lick—it's just a little more complicated and not as easy to spot at first glance. Here, we use a pattern that pulls off two notes up the neck to the open string, add a note on the lower string, then play another pull-off on the string we started with. It sounds a little more convoluted than it is, but look at beats 1–3 of the first measure for a visual. The fact that this pattern lasts three whole beats aids its funkiness as a repeated lick, because the next time through, the pattern then starts on a different beat (beat 4), and it takes three full measures to cycle back through to where the pattern starts on beat 1 again. Play the pattern on the top pair of strings, move down to the second and third strings to play the pattern twice more, and then move down to play the pattern on strings 3–4 and 4–5 once each.

We tie things up by resolving down to the 5th (C) and 3rd (A) of the F chord in the fifth measure and close the phrase by ascending the C major scale followed by an extended C major arpeggio over the C chord in the final two measures.

Try the pick-hand fingerings Atkins would have used, which are shown between the notation and tablature. After the very first pull-off sequence, which he would pick with his thumb, he'd rely on the index finger to pick the first note of every other pull-off. The thumb only plays the single notes on the string below each pull-off.

## Lick 7

Atkins would adapt the previous lick to play over different chords. For instance, here's a very similar lick from "Orange Blossom Special" played out of the same position, but here we're playing over a D–A–E–A progression in the key of A (not in the key of C, as the previous lick was). As you can see, we only need to shift a few notes to make this work in A: move up a half step to the ninth fret for the C# note on the first string and move down a half step for the B and F# notes at the fourth fret of the third and fourth strings, respectively.

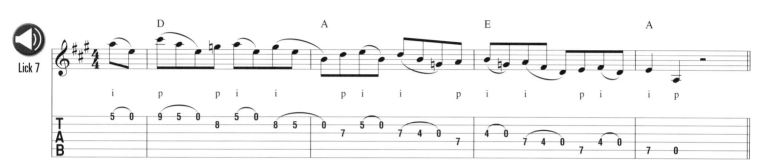

## Lick 8

For this lick, we have a very cool vamp-like sound by playing double stops and pulling off to the open strings. Here, Chet would be thinking about chord shapes as he follows the underlying progression with three-note shapes up the neck, playing these C, D7, and F shapes over the C, D9, and F chords, respectively:

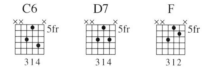

Notice that we hold that last shape—the F chord—*over* the G chord, creating an F/G sound, which is a great resolution to the following C chord.

For the mechanics of the lick itself, the toughest part is plucking the double stop on the second and third strings and then pulling off just the lower one to the open string below. To get a handle on this, isolate just this double stop, the pull-off, and the following note on the fourth string, slow it down, and repeat it until you're comfortable with it.

## Licks Alternating with an Open String

Atkins also alternated between melody notes and open strings to create melodies and licks—a technique sometimes found in classical repertoire. These licks often used the same open string for long stretches, alternating with notes on that same string and other strings, as well.

### Lick 9

This lick is shaped around a D–A–E chord progression in E and alternates melody notes with both the high E and B strings. Notice, however, how it stays with each open string throughout a chord change, spending at least enough time on each one to act as a pedal point. Atkins would pick licks like this by strictly alternating between his thumb and index finger, as shown between the notation and tablature.

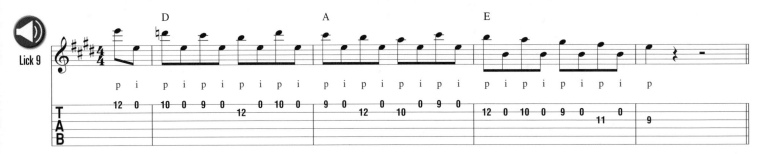

### Lick 10

This lick alternates melody notes with only the high E string. Here, you'll really benefit from strictly alternating between your thumb and index finger because those opposing fingers can naturally spread out to alternate between notes on the fourth and first (or even fifth and first!) strings (which is much more difficult with a pick, for instance.)

Chet plays something similar to this lick in both "Cascade" and "Blue Angel."

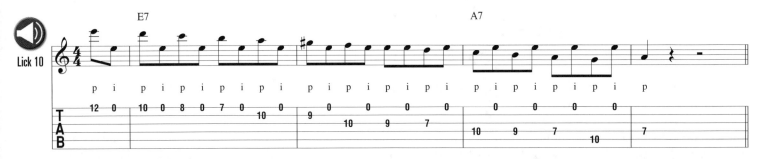

### Lick 11

Here's a lick that dances around the open E string by encircling it with notes above and below it on the E and B strings.

# Arpeggio Licks

Atkins used arpeggios in a number of ways to play different types of licks. Here, we'll look at several that use closed-position arpeggio shapes (no open strings).

## Lick 12

Using a three-fingered rolling pick-hand approach with his thumb, index, and middle fingers, Atkins was able to pick out simple arpeggio licks on three consecutive strings at blinding speeds. Here's a typical passage that uses this approach. As you'd expect, each chord in the A–D–E–A progression is outlined with its corresponding arpeggio. But the harmony is also embellished by adding quick arpeggios of other chords for a little extra motion, such as the A arpeggio superimposed over the D chord in measure 3, and the D arpeggios superimposed over the A chord in measures 7–8.

## Lick 13

This lick shows how Atkins could use a two-string approach to outline a three-note arpeggio by accessing two notes on one string with a pull-off. In this lick, the underlying chord progression is adhered to strictly with corresponding arpeggios for each chord.

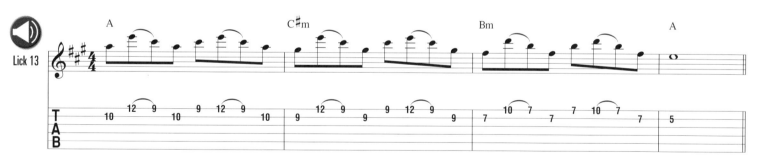

## Arpeggio Licks with Open Strings

When you add open strings to arpeggio licks, things open up quite a bit more because you can use those open strings to free up your fretting hand, which allows you to shift positions while in the middle of the arpeggio—a trick Atkins was quite masterful at. This allows you to play much longer arpeggios than the three-note closed-position licks we just looked at.

## Lick 14

Here's a cascading Em11 arpeggio lick. This one starts down at the lowest note of the guitar, and the shift happens almost at the beginning—just after the first hammer-on at beat 1 of the first full measure. Here, play the hammer-on, and while you're plucking the open fifth string, that buys you some time to shift your hand up to the seventh fret, where it parks for the rest of the lick. Several picking options are shown. Once you get going, it's easier to alternate between the same pair of fingers throughout the rest of the lick: either thumb-index or thumb-middle.

## Lick 15

This G6 lick starts in seventh position but shifts up to 10th position midway through the first measure, moving back down to seventh position midway through the second measure. This one uses more of a rolling p-i-m pattern with the picking fingers (though pay attention to the first note, played with the index finger, and the apex of the run, which begins its descent without the middle finger).

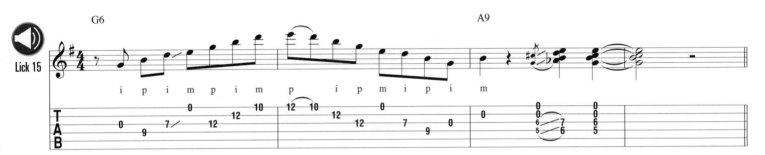

# *Roll Licks*

We've already seen that Atkins incorporates roll patterns into quite a few licks and melody parts that actually don't end up *sounding* like rolls. Here we'll look at a few licks that actually *do* sound like rolls!

## Lick 16

The first lick is simply a basic forward roll pattern on a G arpeggio up the neck, which turns into a G6 chord with the addition of the open E string on top. Atkins played something similar as a fill in the tune "Tiger Rag," and it's essentially the foundation of much of his roll playing; we even use it as the foundation of our roll exploration in the "Stylistic DNA" section of the book. Use a thumb-index-middle picking pattern throughout, alternating your middle finger between the second and first strings:

## Lick 17

Atkins could use the forward-roll pattern in many different ways. Here's a lick down at the nut over a C7–F chord change that demonstrates one variation he could add to this pattern to multiply his options. We alternate between the fifth and fourth strings with the thumb, instead of playing just the fourth string. Notice the downward brush across the strings.

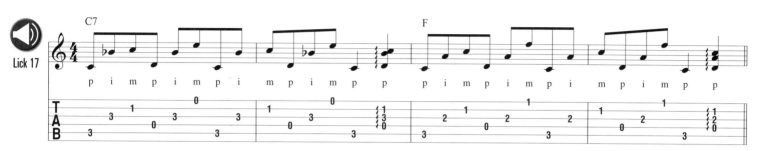

## Lick 18

This one shows a more complicated roll pattern that incorporates a reverse roll into the mix. Here, you start to play a forward roll, but after the thumb and index play, you switch to a reverse roll pattern of p-m-i, which you play twice to complete the half-measure pattern. On top of this, the lick slides two- and three-note chord shapes around on strings 2–4. Here, notice how the shapes are shifted on every beat, meaning that you're playing two chord shapes for each cycle through the roll pattern. Atkins would often do this, though he'd also park on a single chord for a full cycle through the pattern. He played a similar rolling lick to this pattern in his duet version of "Avalon" with Les Paul.

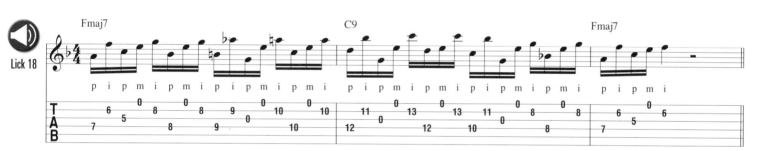

## Lick 19

This one uses the same complicated roll pattern as the previous lick, but here we've created more of a cascading scalar sound simply by fretting an extra note on beat 3 of each measure, playing the open string below every other time we play that string.

# Three-Notes-Per-String Licks

Chet Atkins was fond of three-notes-per-string scale patterns, which is a topic discussed in more detail in the "Stylistic DNA" section. Sometimes these licks would look and sound like cool scalar patterns, as we'll see in the first two licks here. But sometimes he'd dress them up by pausing, moving back and forth, and embellishing them to the point that they're not immediately recognizable as patterns envisioned from a three-notes-per-string foundation, which we'll see in Licks 22 and 23.

### Lick 20

The ascending B Mixolydian scale pattern that kicks off this lick is perhaps Atkins' favorite three-notes-per-string pattern. After cresting the top of the scale pattern in measure 3, we turn around and come back down using a two-note sequence over the E7 chord that continues through the A7 chord in measure 5, finally slowing down to descending quarter notes in measure 6 to arrive at the tonic of D7 by the end of the lick. Use a repeating i-p-m pattern throughout. Or, if it's easier for you to think of the thumb as the first note in a pattern, just start with the index finger and then play a p-m-i pattern throughout.

### Lick 21

This lick uses a descending three-notes-per-string pattern to play a C major scale. It uses the same picking pattern as the previous lick, though this time we start with the thumb.

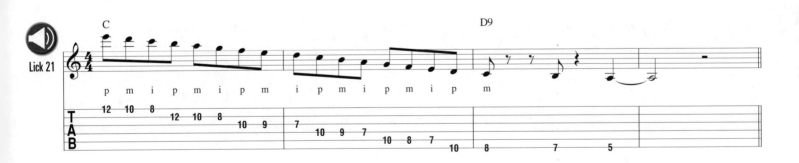

### Lick 22

This two-part lick shows an initial theme in the first measure, which ascends and descends a three-notes-per-string G scale with rhythmic embellishment. The second part takes this initial theme and uses it as a springboard to run up the pattern and climax with a bend and arpeggio on the G chord in measure 4. This is similar to a lick Atkins played in his recording of "Which Way Del Vecchio."

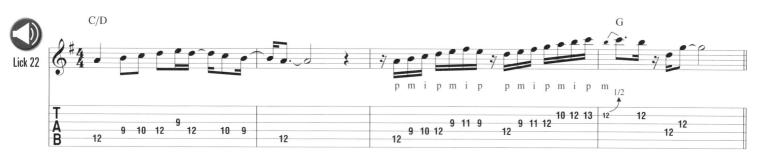

### Lick 23

This lick uses an ascending and accelerating three-notes-per-string Bb major scale for an effective climax and resolution to the Bb chord in the second measure. This one's similar to a lick Atkins played in his cover of Keith Jarrett's "My Song."

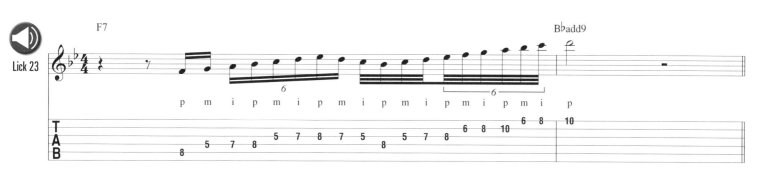

# Sweep-Picking Licks

Whenever he wanted to add a little frenetic fury to his lead lines, Atkins would throw in a sweep-picked lick or two. With the thumbpick firmly in place, he could hold his index finger and thumb together, making his thumbpick feel more like a flatpick, and easily sweep out ascending and descending sweep-picked lines.

### Lick 24

This sweep-picked lick starts on the descent, but watch for the quick pull-off after plucking the first string with a downstroke. Keep your pick moving downward, though, and sweep through the next four strings before pulling off and hammering back on between the 10th and 11th frets down on the fifth string. Coming back up, sweep your pick in a downstroke through the top four strings and finish with the hammer-on.

Atkins would play sweep-picked licks by loosely fretting the shape with his fret hand, but not applying pressure to the notes until just before his pick came in contact with the strings, so that the notes didn't ring together too much. For sweep-picked licks like this, he often needed to access the same fret of consecutive strings; with many more notes than fingers, he'd usually roll his fret hand across several strings to access more than one note with one finger. For this lick, he would roll his index finger, which is the easiest one for most people, since it's the finger you use most often to play a barre.

Here, the lick is shown in the context of an F chord, where it superimposes an F7#9 sound on top, but Atkins was just as likely to use it over Ab for an Abmaj7 sound. He plays a similar dominant-seventh lick in "Please Stay Tuned" and a similar major-seventh lick in "My Song."

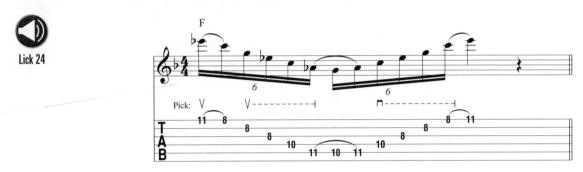

## Lick 25

This lick uses all upstrokes to sweep pick several descending chord shapes, all superimposed over an E chord. Here, you'll need to again pause your pick slightly after the first note for the pull-off, continuing the downward motion until you reach the fifth string, where you'll play the second pull-off. The lick starts with an E arpeggio and then descends through a D arpeggio on beat 3, a C#m arpeggio on beat 4, and lands on a B arpeggio as you reach the B7 chord. You'll need to roll the ring finger of your fretting hand to access the notes on strings 2–4 for the E, D, and B arpeggios. You'll need to roll that same finger for the notes on strings 3 and 4 for the C#m arpeggio on beat 4 of the first measure, as well.

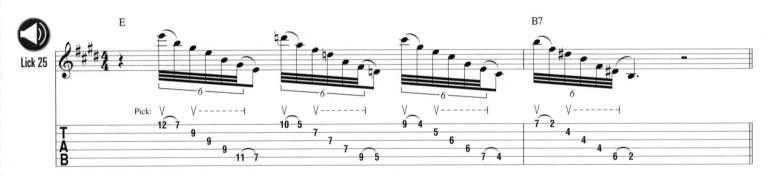

# Licks with Artificial Harmonics

Atkins' unique "harp harmonic" technique, which mixes artificial harmonics with regular notes, was a great way for him to inject a little jaw-dropping technique and sound into a lick. Here are several that exemplify the type of licks he'd create with this technique. The technique involved is explored in detail in the "Essential Techniques" and "Stylistic DNA" sections.

## Lick 26

This one ascends straight up a D major pentatonic scale, alternating between fretted notes and artificial harmonics, before descending several times from the top of the pattern. It then moves up a half step to repeat the same thing over Eb. Atkins played similar licks in the opening of "White Christmas" and "When You Wish upon a Star."

## Lick 27

This lick incorporates pull-offs to create even more of a step-wise scalar sound. Atkins spoke of how he first recorded a lick similar to the previous one, and when Lenny Breau heard the technique, he learned it and incorporated pull-offs like this into his playing, which Chet then started to do, as well.

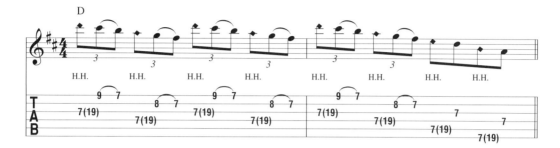

# Unusual Licks

Atkins occasionally pulled something crazy out of his bag of tricks. Here we'll look at several unusual licks that use discordant sounds to create tension and release, as well as a tapping lick!

## Lick 28

Here's a discordant lick Atkins might have played over a G chord. We're using the same three-note pattern to ascend through all the strings. Using one finger per fret, align your index, middle, and ring fingers on frets 3, 4, and 5, respectively. Then, fret the sixth string with your index finger, the fifth string with your middle finger, and the fourth string with your ring finger, creating a discordant tritone between the two root notes on bottom and top. Next, move this up a string set, which creates even more discord, and continue shifting the pattern up each string set until you reach the first string. To finish, pull off to the third-fret G note, which is a nice resolution to the root after all of that discord!

## Lick 29

In contrast to the tritone discord found in the previous lick, this one creates discord by playing pairs of notes a half step away from each other to create clusters of tension that we resolve at the end by plucking the low root G of the underlying chord. Again, we're using three-note groupings, though the pattern isn't as strict as in the previous lick. For the first set of notes, you'll need to barre the third fret of the first and second strings with your index finger and reach over with your pinky to fret the sixth fret of the third string. Then, for the second sequence of notes, roll your index finger up to fret the third fret of the third string and leave the first and second strings open. Then the lick simply transfers this pattern down a string set. But to keep that half-step tension going, you'll have to move over to the fourth fret of the fourth string (since the distance between the third and fourth strings is a half step greater than it is between the second and third strings). Repeat the pattern again, down one more string set, and finish with that third-fret root G note.

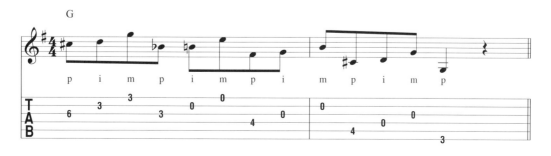

## Lick 30

While many folks affiliate tapping with big-hair bands and metal, Atkins actually threw in a tapping lick in his 1981 recording of "Orange Blossom Special" from *Country After All These Years.* While Eddie Van Halen had already arrived on the scene with the release of Van Halen's eponymous debut in 1978, this is still a surprise from Chet. Here's a similar line that follows the chord progression, using one string to arpeggiate each chord. We start by plucking the string with the pick-hand index finger, but not as you would normally pluck a string. Here, we hold it over the 12th fret, bringing it down as if to tap the note, but instead of tapping it, simply push down enough on the string to get a purchase on it, and without sounding a note, pull off to the open string. We then use the fret-hand index and pinky fingers for the hammer-ons at the fourth and seventh fret, respectively, and the index finger of our picking hand to alternate taps at the 12th and ninth frets, which sound the root and 6th of an A chord, respectively. Notice when we transfer up to the D chord, we shift our index finger up an eighth note early, so that we tap the ninth fret of the fourth string (instead of finishing the A6 arpeggio). This helps to easily start the upcoming D arpeggio by pulling off from that note. Over the D chord, repeat the same lick, only on the fourth string. Over the E chord, we repeat it again down on the low E string. (Remember to reach down and tap the ninth fret one note early again as you switch to the E chord.) We finish up tapping the A arpeggio on the fifth string for the A chord again.

# SIGNATURE PHRASES AND PASSAGES

In this section, we'll take a look at ten excerpts that showcase Atkins' unique technical and stylistic talents within the context of either a short phrase or a longer passage. Whether he was playing melodies over alternate-bass fingerpicking, lighting up the fretboard with quick cascading harmonics, playfully embellishing a song with the vibrato bar, or picking out blinding roll patterns, Atkins left his signature on a huge and wide-ranging library of great music.

## *Windy and Warm*
### Alternate-Bass Fingerpicking

Chet first recorded the John Loudermilk song "Windy and Warm" on nylon-string guitar for a single release in 1961. But his version on electric, included on the 1962 album *Down Home*, has become the classic version of the song.

The main theme of the song is a great example and introductory study of Atkins' alternate-bass picking against a melody. Here, Atkins picks out a single-note line on top of his alternate-bass fingerpicking, and each of these parts sounds like a separate instrument. As we discuss in the upcoming "Essential Techniques" section (as well as in some of the full song transcriptions), Atkins helps achieved this separation by palm muting *only* the bass part, which is played by the thumb. This naturally pushes the bass into the background, giving it a thumping and percussive bass-like sound, while also pushing the ringing melodies on top into the forefront.

This is a simple passage, but it's not as easy as it sounds, since you have to master the subtleties of palm muting with alternate-bass fingerpicking to bring it to life. One way to help you separate the bass from the melody is to physically learn them separately before putting them together. First, try picking out the upstemmed melody with your fingers. For the half-step bend in the second measure, your hand may naturally want to slide up so you can grab it with your stronger ring finger. But if you use your pinky, your hand will still be in the Am chord position for the end of the measure. You can bring your ring finger up to help support the bend, which should make things a bit easier, and this is exactly what Atkins does. This briefly means his middle finger comes up, too, and that's why we hear the open D-string bass note on beat 2 of the measure; Atkins has lifted that finger off briefly. But it's quite easy to recover from this minor adjustment and bring your hand back down in place over the Am chord. The two-fret slide at the beginning of the fourth measure is another place where many folks feel most comfortable using the ring finger, but Atkins again uses his pinky finger here. However, he uses his index finger on the high E string—the same finger you'd use if you employed your ring finger for that slide.

To get yourself ready for the palm-muted bass part, practice the melody while holding your palm in place, muting the bass strings. Practice rolling that palm down even a bit more, just to see how far you have to go before you start choking the melody; then roll it back. Now your hand has a sense of how it feels to mute just enough of the strings.

Next, try picking through just the downstemmed bass notes with your thumb, making sure to palm mute every note on the bottom three strings. This is where the exercise gets a little trickier, because you'll notice as you start to get through it that the thumb actually picks through both the fourth and third strings on occasion. Atkins is so precise with his palm muting that when this happens, it almost sounds as if there's another melody note popping out of the mix, but the bass note is still muted. This happens in the last measure of both Letters A and B. When you reach one of these measures, make sure that when that thumb hits both of these strings you can hear a distinct difference between each string; the note on the fourth string should sound muffled and decay quickly, while the note on the third string should ring out. Once you've mastered this subtle move, you're ready to put the two parts together.

**Editorial Note**: On the recording, Chet played this song with a capo on fret 3, causing the song to sound a minor 3rd higher in the key of C minor. It sounds fine in A minor too, but if you want to play along with the recording, simply use a capo on fret 3.

Windy and Warm
Excerpt

Capo III

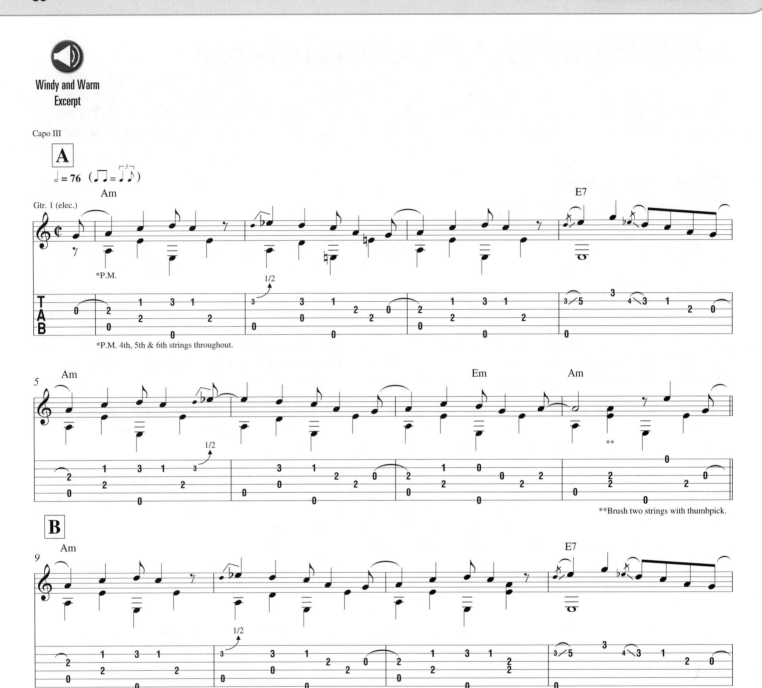

*P.M. 4th, 5th & 6th strings throughout.

**Brush two strings with thumbpick.

# *Trambone*
## Vibrato Bar Usage, Alternate-Bass Fingerpicking

Chet Atkins first released "Trambone" as a single in 1956, and the song also later popped up on his 1962 release, *Down Home*, as well as a host of other compilations over the years. The "head" of this song (the melody) makes great use of the vibrato bar to swoop into the first bass note of each chord from underneath. Perhaps it's this sliding effect in the lower register that made Atkins think of a trombone, since it has a similar sound to a valveless trombone sliding between notes.

The "Trambone" melody section takes Atkins' alternate-bass fingerpicking from "Windy and Warm" to another level with the addition of vibrato bar embellishments. He does a "pre-dive" with the bar to lower the pitch of the strings by a half step *before* striking the first bass note of each chord, plucks the note, and then releases the bar so that the pitch returns to normal on the downbeat of each measure. A pre-dive like this can be a little tricky to nail at first, so a good way to work up to this is by starting with a regular dive, where you play a note *before* you push on the vibrato bar, and then you lower it and raise it again. We'll try this out with the C note at the beginning, but we'll start by picking our note on beat 3, pushing on the vibrato bar to move the pitch down to B for beat 4, and releasing it so it returns to C on beat 1:

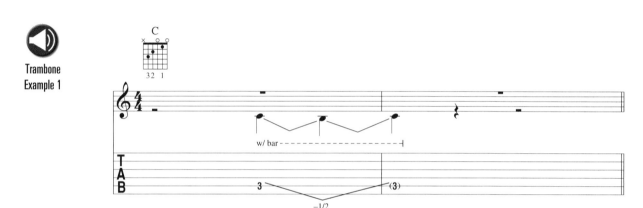

Trambone
Example 1

If you need a reference pitch to shoot for, play the second-fret B note on the fifth string before you start the example and try to keep that in your mind as you start the dive. Unfortunately, you can't really use a reference pitch once you've started your dive, because all of the strings move down in pitch as you push down on the vibrato bar, so none of them are in perfect tune anymore! But this is a great ear-training exercise. Also, make sure you fret the whole C chord with your fretting hand as you do this. Once you start playing the song, you'll need your hand in place to immediately pick the notes accessible from that C shape, so you might as well have your hand in place and ready to go even as we're practicing this dive. Go back and do it like this if you didn't already. If you want to increase your practicing efficiency, you can even loop the example, like this:

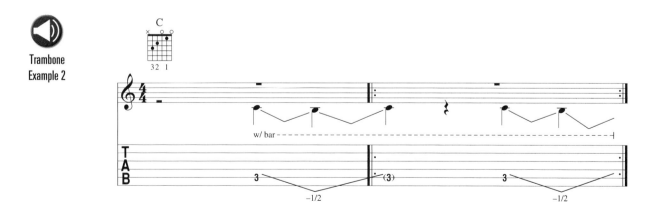

Trambone
Example 2

Pay close attention to *how far* you have to push the vibrato bar down. Once you're comfortable with this motion and the target pitch, try the pre-dive. Here, you'll push down on the bar exactly the same distance, but you'll wait to pick the string until you've reached that target pitch (well, really the target *distance* that your hand holding the bar has become familiar with, since we won't hear the pitch before playing the string). Pluck the string on beat 4 and release again into beat 1 of the next measure:

Trambone
Example 3

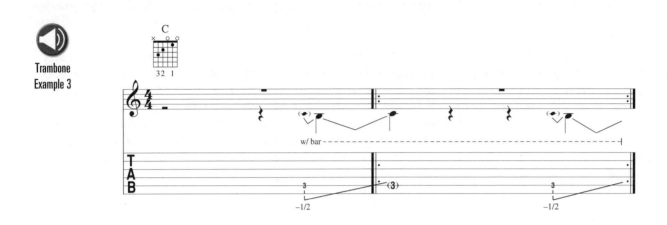

Listen closely to that target pitch as you pluck the note and adjust the bar down or up a little, if necessary, until you nail it. Then, go back and try to pre-dive to the right place again before plucking the string until you eventually get it. Once you're comfortable with this, you're ready to add in the picking:

Trambone
Example 4

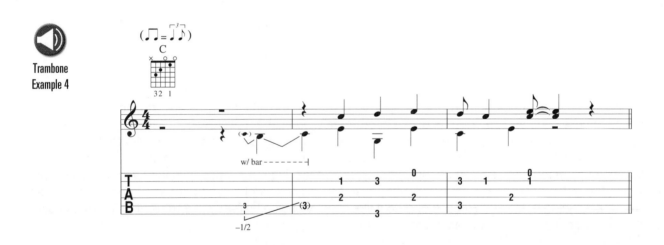

Now that you have that half-step pre-dive down, your hand should be ready for the complete 16-bar section, because all of the pre-dives here are the same distance (half step). If any of them sound a little funny as you play them, stop and isolate them, and go through the previous steps, if necessary, to get them tuned up.

In the final two bars, Atkins plays a nice arpeggio lick that uses a thumb-index-middle (p-i-m) pattern throughout. One of his favorite ways to come up with cool licks was using a bite-sized picking pattern like this and moving it up and down to different string sets. Here, he starts by picking p-i-m on the bottom three strings, moves up a string to repeat it, and finally moves up one more string set to finish the lick on strings 4–2. You can familiarize your fingers with this moving picking pattern by just plucking the open strings in order:

Trambone
Example 5

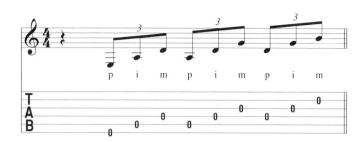

But the trick to this particular lick comes with the hammer-on he adds on the lowest string from E to G, which shifts the pattern over an eighth note and pushes your *middle* finger onto the beat, instead of your thumb—which feels a little different. So, if you think of it as an m-p-i pattern, and practice it like this, it might help you get the hang of it a little more:

Trambone
Example 6

When you have it down, go back and add your thumb pluck and hammer-on back in.

Trambone
Example 7

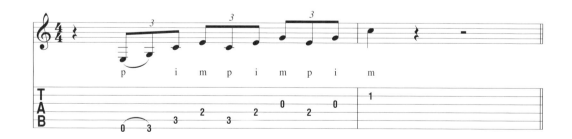

Now you're ready for the entire passage!

Trambone
Excerpt

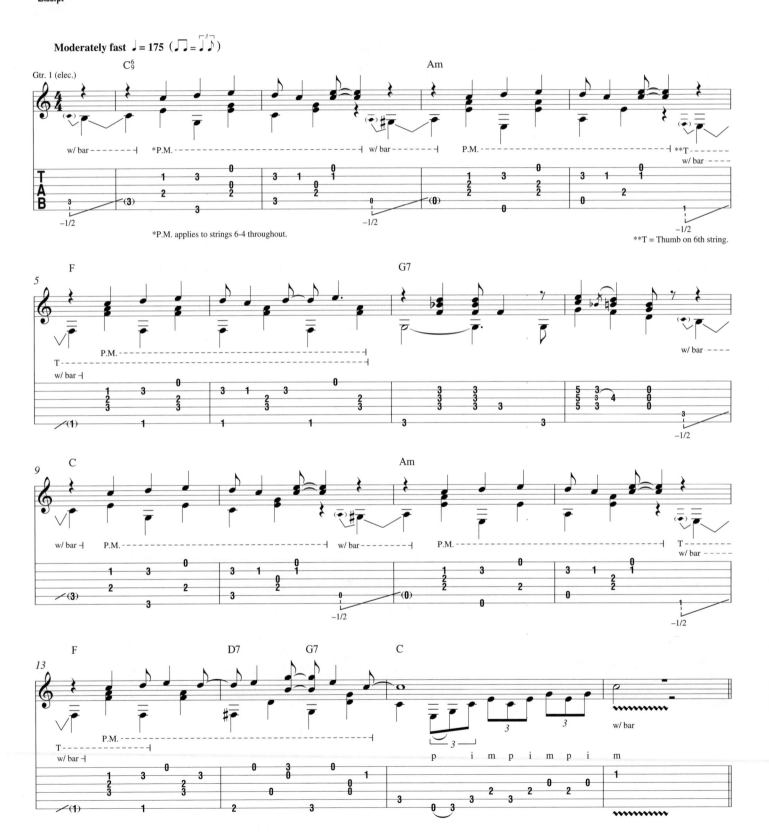

# Blue Angel
## Alternating Melodies Against Open Strings

"Blue Angel" was released both as a single in 1968 and included on the *Hometown* record from the same year. The song was penned by Brazilian guitarist Natalicio Lima, and the opening melody showcases a technique Chet was fond of—alternating melody notes against the static open high E string in a classical manner.

The melody of this excerpt takes advantage of several different minor-scale forms in the key of Am, but the predominant sound comes from the A harmonic minor scale, which uses just one sharped note—G♯:

**Blue Angel
Example 1**

You can see this scale at use in measures 1–5 and 9–15. In measure 6, you'll notice a slight difference, though, because that G♯ has been replaced by a G natural. That's because the background harmony now changes to Em. When we played that G♯ note, there was an E7 chord in the harmony—a major (or dominant) chord that uses a G♯. But an Em chord has a G natural, and we'll match this with our melody, which also means we're now using a standard A natural minor scale:

**Blue Angel
Example 2**

This Em chord in measure 6 acts as a bit of a pivot, because it *sounds* as if we're heading toward the key of Em in the next two measures, with a brief V–i (B7–Em) resolution to Em. Because of that brief tonal shift, the melody now shifts to E harmonic minor, which uses F♯ and D♯:

**Blue Angel
Example 3**

Atkins highlights this subtle tonal shift by surrounding that E note in measure 8 with its upper and lower neighbor tones, both a half step away. This creates even more of a feeling that we've arrived in the key of E minor, but it's really just a passing hint at E minor, as the song jumps straight back into A minor with the A harmonic minor scale and same chord progression that started the piece.

The key to this passage is really in the picking hand, though, where Atkins alternated between his thumb and index finger to pick out these melodic lines. Try this out on the open first string to get a feel for it at first:

**Blue Angel
Example 4**

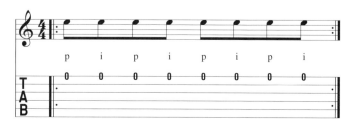

But Atkins alternated fretted notes with the open string, so next try playing an ascending scale on the first string that alternates with the open string. We'll use the A harmonic minor scale to keep to the foundation of the song. (We're starting in the middle of the scale here, since the E note comes first on that string.)

**Blue Angel
Example 5**

The fret-hand fingering isn't quite as important here, because you have time to move your fretting hand each time you pluck an open string (which is every other note!). So find what's most comfortable for you.

You'll notice as you pick through that this is a little different than plucking just notes on the open string or fretted notes. That's because when you play two fretted notes in a row, the string stays in pretty much the same "vertical space" in relation to your picking finger, but when you fret a note and then release the string for an open-string note, the string moves *up* a bit more. Then, when you play the next fretted note, the string moves back down a bit more than your hand may be prepared for.

It's a subtle shift, but it can throw your picking hand off a little, so keep this in mind as you play through the example and the song. The thumb-index picking pattern becomes especially advantageous when you hit the third and fourth measures, as the melody notes walk farther away from the open E string, requiring you to skip one or two strings between picked notes. First play the following measures with the thumb-index combination and then try using a flatpick (or just your thumbpick) to see how much more precisely and quickly you can play it with the alternate thumb-index method:

**Blue Angel
Example 6**

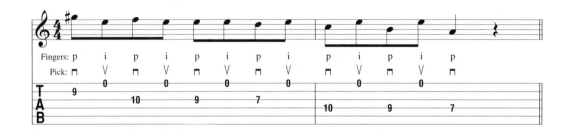

There are, however, places where this approach becomes a little tricky—especially where the thumb or index finger must cross over the other finger to get a string. For instance, in measures 12–13, your index finger crosses under your thumb to play a lower string several times—on the "and" of beat 3 in measure 12, and on the "and" of beats 1 and 4 of measure 13. Your thumb also crosses under your index finger on beat 2 of measure 13. Or, looking at it another way, your thumb *stays* on the higher string as your index finger crosses underneath.

**Blue Angel
Example 7**

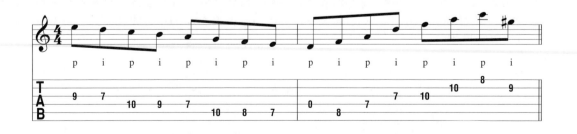

You may need to spend a little more time mastering this passage because of this fingering quirkiness, so slow it down if you need to and then gradually speed it up to performance tempo after you get comfortable with it. Use a capo at the first fret if you want to play along with the recording.

**Blue Angel**
Excerpt

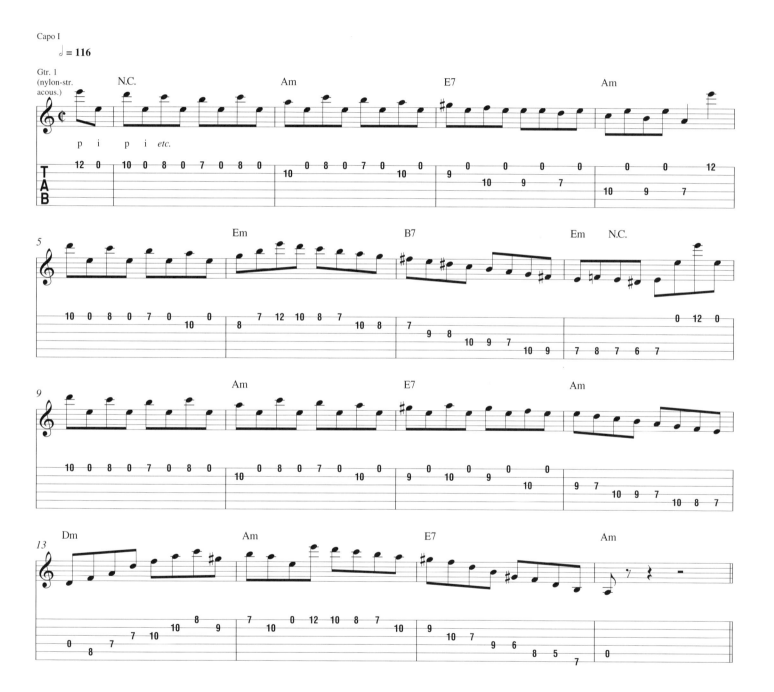

# Cascade
## Rolls

"Cascade" appeared on Chet Atkins' 1977 release, *Me and My Guitar*, aptly demonstrating Chet's ability to mix nylon-string guitar with blazing rolls and licks. The following passage, which is the melody of the song, is a great example of Atkins adapting uptempo rolls from the banjo to the guitar—a technique he used well and often.

In this section, Atkins uses the thumb-index-middle (p-i-m) forward roll pattern that's a popular one on fingerpicking guitar, and it also happened to be one of his favorites. As we've seen in other songs, he uses his thumb and index finger on the fourth and third strings, respectively, while he alternates his index finger between the second and first strings for each roll. After playing the roll four times, he stops midway through the second measure and brushes the top strings with the back of his fingers. This downward string strike, often called a "frail," is another technique lifted from the banjo—along with the roll patterns.

Cascade
Example 1

Atkins basically repeats this roll pattern throughout the whole excerpt, but this first roll over the C6 chord is by far the toughest because of the stretch in the fretting hand. If you have trouble with this, you can try working into it by starting with a capo on the fifth fret (or higher) where the frets are closer together, making the stretches easier. Then try sliding the capo gradually down the fretboard to see if you can play it in root position. But don't push it! Some people's hands simply aren't big enough for this stretch, and you don't want to develop tendonitis. If you find it still too tough, you could tune your guitar down a whole step and capo at the second fret, which would result in the same pitches. If this is still too difficult, you could try playing it in a different key by capoing higher up the neck.

He uses his index finger on the third string, with only two small exceptions. The first happens in measures 7–8, where he plucks the high C note in the double stop C/E with that index finger, which moves it up to the second string (the thumb plays the bottom note). Then, he keeps that index finger up on the second string for the following slide up and down the top two strings, which he plucks with his index and middle fingers, as shown below.

Cascade
Example 2

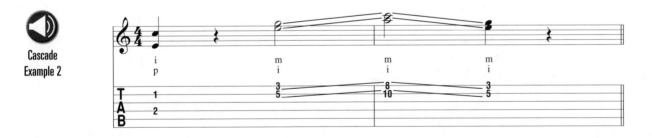

The final two measures also feature his index finger up on the second string. These two measures also mark the only time his thumb comes up from the fourth string. Here, he picks 6th intervals with his thumb and index finger on strings 4 and 2, respectively, but moves that thumb up to grab the pair of notes on strings 3 and 1 with the thumb and middle finger, respectively:

Cascade
Example 3

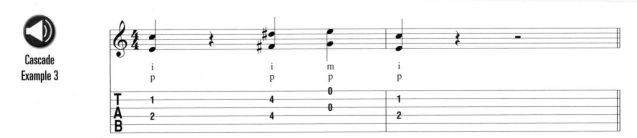

Here's the full 16-bar melody:

Cascade
Excerpt

# *Chinatown, My Chinatown*
## Artificial Harmonics in Dyads and Chords

Chet Atkins recorded "Chinatown, My Chinatown" way back in 1952, and it has made its way onto quite a number of compilation recordings since then. Atkins was a master of artificial harmonics, and on the second time through the melody, he clearly demonstrates this. Here, he plays the melody with double stops that pair a standard note with an artificial harmonic, specifically using the harp harmonic technique.

To play these note pairs (measures 1–19), Atkins plays mostly 6th and 3rd intervals on the top four strings (with the occasional 7th or 4th). Here's the first phrase played as standard notes:

Chinatown
Example 1

To create his harmonic line, Atkins uses the harp harmonic technique to play an artificial harmonic on the *lower* note in each pair. This pops the lower note up an octave, which is *higher* than the pitch he's playing on the higher string, essentially inverting those intervals—i.e., it turns a 6th into a 3rd, etc. Realize that this is the same technique he used to create all those cascading scale licks (see the transcription of "Cannon Ball Rag" or the "Essential Techniques" chapter for more on this), it's just that he's using it here to create harmonized double-stops or single-note phrases.

Chinatown
Example 2

To perform these double stops with an artificial harmonic, it requires *three fingers* on your picking hand. Your index finger lightly touches the string 12 frets above the note from which you want to generate a harmonic, and then you pluck that note with the thumb, behind the index finger (closer to the bridge). You're also simultaneously plucking the higher string with your middle (or ring) finger. Here's how your pick hand should look just before plucking the first pair of notes:

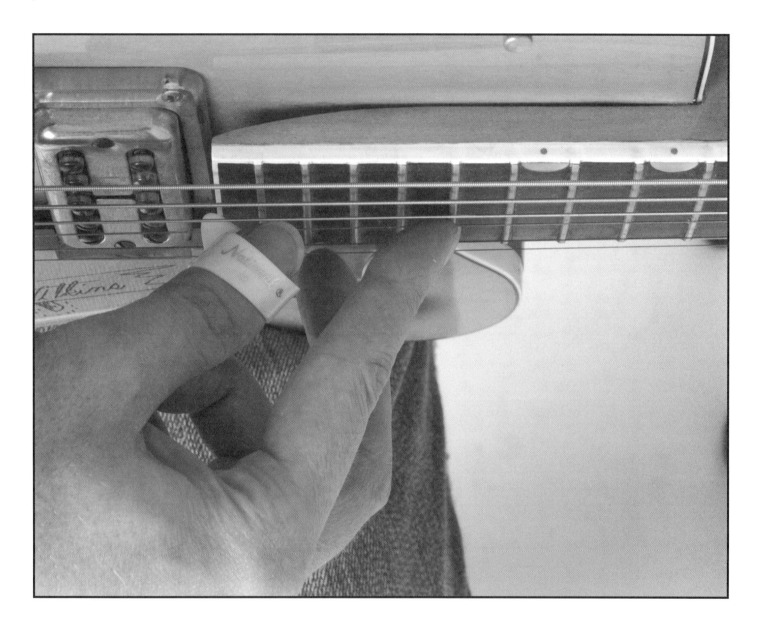

Throughout this passage, you'll need to especially focus on using that pick-hand index finger to mirror the position of the fretted note below, just 12 frets up. Focus on moving your middle finger between the top two strings as you go, but you don't need to worry at all about its placement horizontally along the string (as you do for that index finger). So just let that middle finger come along for the ride and pluck the string wherever it ends up, horizontally. For the bent strings in measures 8–11 and 16, just play the double stop and harmonic as you would normally and then bend the strings up. The chiming harmonic will bend up, as well.

At measure 20, Atkins breaks into a single-note line that generally picks up a little speed. Here, you don't have to focus on the mechanics of a double stop and artificial harmonic together, which makes it a little easier in that sense. But now the line moves around the frets a little more quickly, so you'll need to focus on following along with your pick-hand index finger a little more carefully. For the hammer-on and pull-off in measure 20, just play the harmonic for the first note, and hammer and pull off on the lower frets with your fret hand. Again, the harmonic will continue to sound as if it's being hammered and pulled an octave higher. And when you reach the pre-bend in measure 29, again, just pluck the string 12 frets higher than the *unbent* string—at the 19th fret (instead of trying to move up between the frets to make up for the bend raising the pitch).

Chinatown
Excerpt

# Cascade
## Cascading Harp Harmonics

"Cascade" features a wide array of Atkins' favorite techniques, from rolls to hot licks, but it also features eight bars of his unique cascading harp harmonics, which are highlighted in the following excerpt. As we've seen in some of the complete songs (and will explore in the following "Stylistic DNA" section), he often did this in one of two ways: by either working out of fretted chord shapes, or by barring across the strings while accessing nearby notes to create scalar-type passages. Here, he uses the latter concept by barring across the first four strings at the fifth fret and operating from this position via pull-offs and artificial harmonics to create these flowing scalar lines:

From this C6 (or Am7) chord, he creates a descending line from the C major scale in this octave:

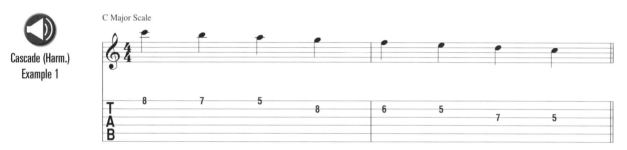

Cascade (Harm.)
Example 1

When shown the two previous examples, many guitarists' first instinct would be to simply play the line via a series of pull-offs on the top two strings:

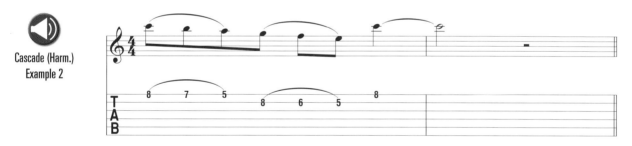

Cascade (Harm.)
Example 2

Atkins' method is considerably more difficult, but the payoff is huge: a thick, ringing harmonic passage (as opposed to simply a series of pull-offs). By bringing the notes on the lower two strings up an octave via artifical harmonics, he can then fill in the cracks of the scale by accessing notes around the shape via pull-offs on the top two strings. First, practice the line without the harmonics, using your thumb to pick the notes on the third and fourth strings and your *middle finger* (or ring finger) to pick the notes on the first two strings. It's key that you use your middle or ring finger here, because you'll need that index finger for the artificial harmonics.

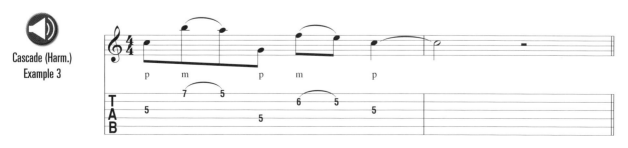

Cascade (Harm.)
Example 3

Once your thumb and middle finger are comfortable alternating between their strings, try just the harmonics. Keep that fret-hand index finger barred across the fifth fret, lightly touch the string with your pick-hand index finger 12 frets above the barre (the 17th fret) for whichever string you want to pick, and pluck the string with your thumb behind that index finger.

Now try just the harmonics in the line:

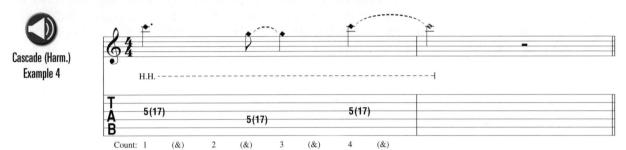

Cascade (Harm.)
Example 4

You can count along to keep yourself picking these notes in the right places (every third eighth note), but we're not as concerned here with playing it in time, so don't worry too much about that. We're more concerned about playing the harmonics on two adjacent strings. When you add the other notes back in, you'll naturally feel the beat a little more strongly, since there will be a note played for every eighth-note subdivision. Once you have this down, you're ready to integrate the parts into one and play the full passage:

Cascade (Harm.)
Excerpt

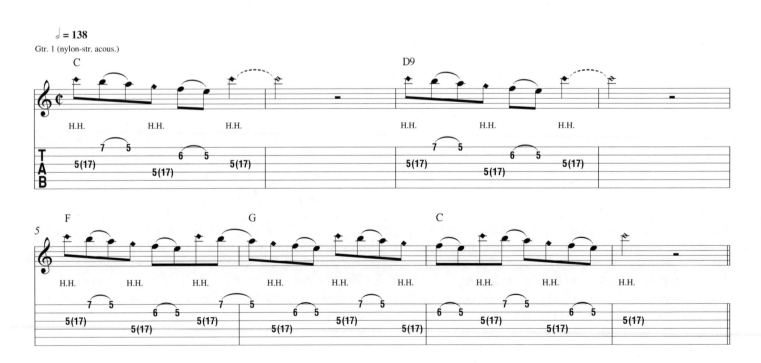

# *Galloping on the Guitar*
## Mixing Fretted Notes up the Neck with Open Strings

"Galloping on the Guitar" was one of Atkins' earlier recordings, having been recorded and released as a single in 1952, but it was also included on his first full-length recording in 1952, *Gallopin' Guitar.* Chet was brilliant at mixing fretted notes up the neck with the open strings to create licks, melodies, and scale patterns, and the melody of "Galloping on the Guitar" is a great example of this.

Atkins uses just the thumb and index finger of his picking hand to play this entire excerpt from "Galloping on the Guitar." For the single-note lines, he alternates between his thumb and index finger throughout the line, like this:

Galloping Example 1

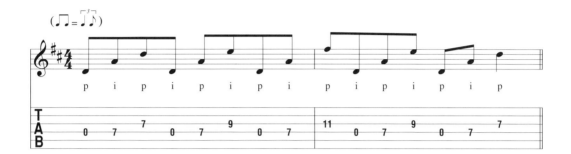

This gets a bit more difficult when you start to play across more than two strings, because the thumb and index finger end up crossing a bit (the thumb playing higher strings while the index finger plays lower strings). This happens especially in measures 2–4, so pay careful attention to those areas where the thumb and finger crosses (in measure 4 on the "and" of beat 1 and on beat 4).

Galloping Example 2

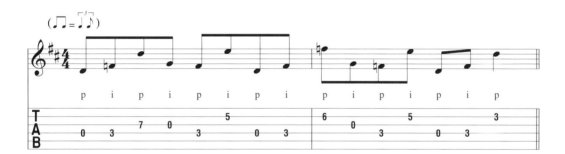

For the double stops and double-stop bends in the final two measures of each eight-bar phrase, Atkins picks the lower note with his thumb and the higher note with his index finger, filling in any single-note lines in between by alternating again with the thumb and index finger:

Galloping Example 3

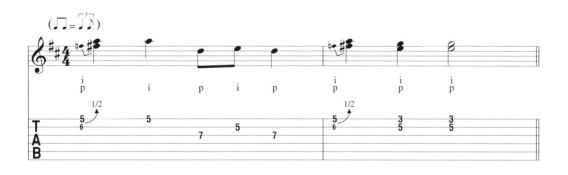

For the fretting hand, Atkins flattened his index finger, quickly rolling it to fret *both* notes on the seventh fret in measures 1 and 2. To try this out, start with the tip of your index finger on the seventh fret of the fourth string but angle it into the fretboard a little more than normal (so that it's not going closer to straight into the fretboard as it normally would). After plucking the note on that string, quickly roll the finger so that the pad between the tip and first knuckle frets the third string while simultaneously letting pressure off of the fourth string (and dampening it in the process).

It's a bit of a stretch to keep your hand in position and reach up for the 11th fret with your pinky at the beginning of measure 2, but not so tough because it's so far up the neck where the frets are closer together. However, when the line is transposed down closer to the nut over the G chord, notice how Atkins plays it across more strings so that he doesn't have to stretch as far for that highest note.

Galloping
Excerpt

# *Black Mountain Rag*
## Cascading Pull-Offs

About half a minute from the end of Chet Atkins' vintage recording of "Black Mountain Rag," he plays an extended series of cascading triplet pull-offs to the open strings at the nut of his guitar. This technique was one of his favorites, and it crops up in many tunes as a quick fill, but here it acts as a little bit more of an extended passage. Note that Atkins played this version of "Black Mountain Rag" in open G tuning (D–G–D–G–B–D) with a capo on the first fret, so make sure you're in the right tuning before you dive into the examples! The capo is only necessary if you want to play along with the recording, though it probably does help a little bit with executing the fast pull-offs as well. Examples 1 and 2 below are played without a capo on the accompanying audio, but the full excerpt is capoed to match Chet's original recording.

Whenever Chet played this type of run, he'd align his fingers in a one-finger-per-fret position down near the nut of his guitar, with his index finger usually at the first or second fret. For this particular passage, he lines that index finger up at the first fret, with the middle, ring, and pinky falling into place at the second, third, and fourth frets, respectively.

For the run, then, play the hammer-on pickup with your index and middle fingers:

Black Mountain Rag
Example 1

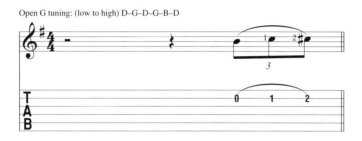

And for the following pull-offs, use your ring and middle fingers, in that order:

Black Mountain Rag
Example 2

This is quite a workout for your middle and ring fingers, since they play *every* pull-off in this whole passage. It's tough enough to play a pull-off lick like this at the blinding speed Atkins did, but on this tune, he also plays an alternate-bass pattern under most of the pull-offs! First, practice the pull-offs on their own to get them under your fingers. Then try adding the alternate-bass line underneath once you're comfortable with it.

Atkins often played pull-off patterns without the alternating bass, which makes for a great fill, and that's exactly what he does here in the final two measures (measures 7–8). Since he had the thumb going in the earlier measures, he needed to pick the first note of each pull-off with his index or middle finger, but when he played pull-offs without the bass underneath, he used his thumb to pluck all of these first notes, which adds a little extra punch. Here, your fret-hand fingers finally move up to the first string and play down through strings 1–3 and then strings 2–4 before punctuating with a solid thumb pluck on beat 3 of the final measure.

**Black Mountain Rag**
Excerpt

Open G tuning, capo I: (low to high) D–G–D–G–B–D

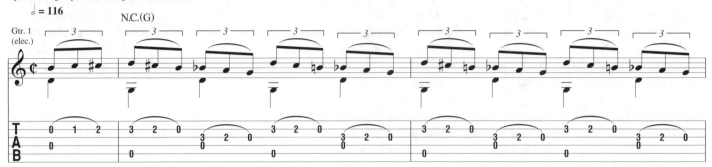

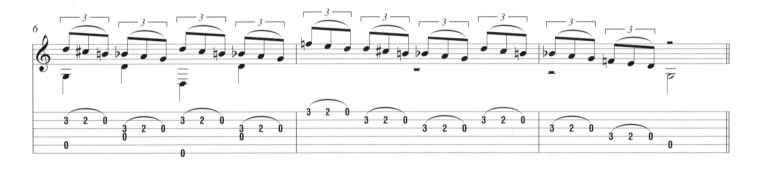

# Alabama Jubilee
## Alternate-Bass Lead

While many think of alternate-bass fingerpicking as solely a backup device, or a backup technique with melody on top, Atkins would sometimes use it as a way to play barn-burning lead licks. His recording of "Alabama Jubilee" from his 1954 release, *A Session with Chet Atkins*, has a great example of this in an extended passage near the two-minute mark of the song.

When Atkins played these passages, he wouldn't park on a chord shape throughout its corresponding harmony. Instead, he'd generally pick a chord shape just *once*, quickly moving through other chord inversions and passing chords every half measure (in cut time; in a slower four where he picked out sixteenth notes, he'd switch chords *every beat!*). Because this required some incredibly swift chord switching in the fretting hand, Atkins wouldn't fret full chords—just the three or four notes he'd use to outline each one. For instance, instead of the A and Dm shapes shown on the left of each group, he'd opt for their streamlined versions, shown to the right.

Putting a few shapes into the context of a line with alternate-bass picking, here's how he might move from a root-position A chord up to a first-inversion A/C♯ chord several frets higher.

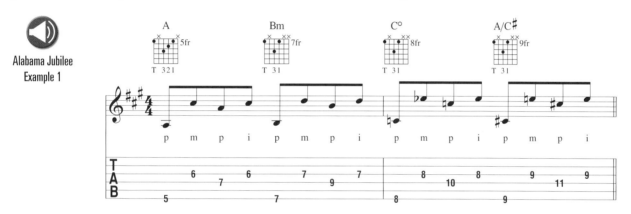

**Alabama Jubilee
Example 1**

One of the beauties of using small three-note shapes like this is that one shape can imply many chords. For instance, the C° chord in the previous example could simply be thought of as a passing A♭/C chord—a chromatic chord one half step below the A/C♯ that's slid up to resolve on the A/C♯. Alternatively, you could think of *all* of those last three chords as the same chord shape (which they are), slid up by a half step; so in a different context, it might sound like Bm–Cm–C♯m.

Atkins generally used a p–m–p–i pattern for these licks, which helped facilitate the speediness at which he could play them. However, when you speed that previous example up to the fiery tempo Atkins might play it at, you'll notice that it gets incredibly difficult to play the last note of each shape cleanly and change chord shapes in time to be ready for that first thumb pluck of the next shape. So Atkins remedied this problem the way Merle Travis would: by simply changing shapes while his index finger was plucking its string—which more often than not ended up being the open G string. So, here's how that previous passage would look:

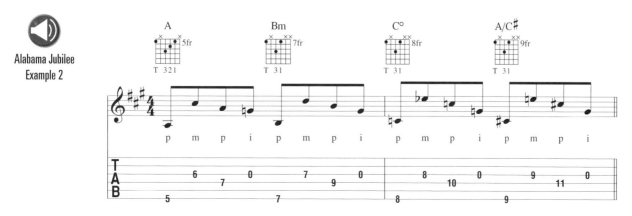

**Alabama Jubilee
Example 2**

Once you're comfortable with the previous example and can change chords at a brisk tempo, you're ready for the full passage:

Alabama Jubilee
Excerpt

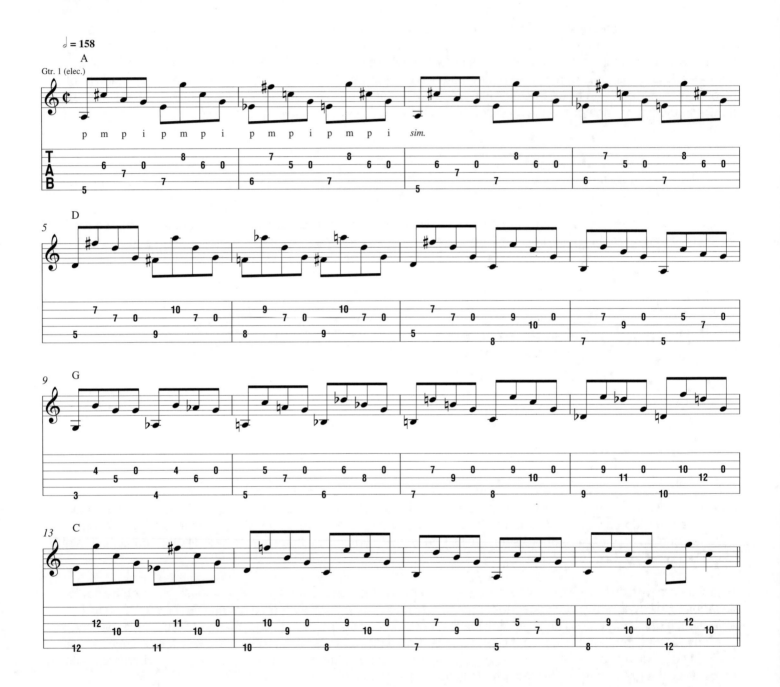

Words by Jack Yellen
Music by George Cobb
Copyright © 2014 by HAL LEONARD CORPORATION
International Copyright Secured   All Rights Reserved

# Down Hill Drag
## Chord-Melody Playing

Atkins was fond of playing melodies in a stripped-down chord-melody style using two- or three-note chord shapes on the treble strings, and the melody of his early recording, "Down Hill Drag," is a great example of this. After a bass-note pickup, Atkins frets the only full barre chord of the melody—a C chord at the eighth fret—with his thumb wrapped around the neck of the guitar to get the bottom note:

After this chord, he uses the top three notes of this shape and its minor counterpart, along with several other three-note shapes on strings 1–3 and 2–4, to play the first four measures of the melody. (Note that the third shape could be considered either a minor triad or a sixth chord in the context of this piece. At the nut, it would be either Dm or F6; at the sixth fret, as in measure 2 of the excerpt, it would be either a Gm or B♭6.)

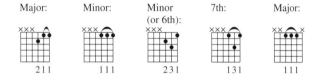

Over the F, G, and C chords in measures 5–10, Atkins plays just the following shapes, which are used to imply major, dominant, and passing sounds over the F and G chords, and a major chord over the C:

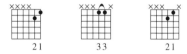

At measure 12, he repeats the initial pickup but adds an octave note for each of the pickup notes, and the melody repeats itself in measures 13–24.

Most of the second section (measures 25–40) comes out of just the following three shapes, which he slides down a half step for embellishment. However, for the first two shapes, it's much easier to only fret the top three strings of each shape when you're sliding around and only add the lowest string when you have to play it. For instance, for the C chord, you'd only add that string on beat 3 of measures 25–26 and 33–35.

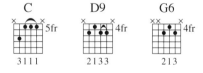

Aside from those three shapes, Atkins only uses the following C triad at the nut (measures 31 and 39) and these two dominant A chords up the neck in measures 28 (the A7) and 36 (the A9):

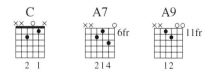

Once you have these shapes under your fingers, you're ready to tackle the complete passage.

**Down Hill Drag**
Excerpt

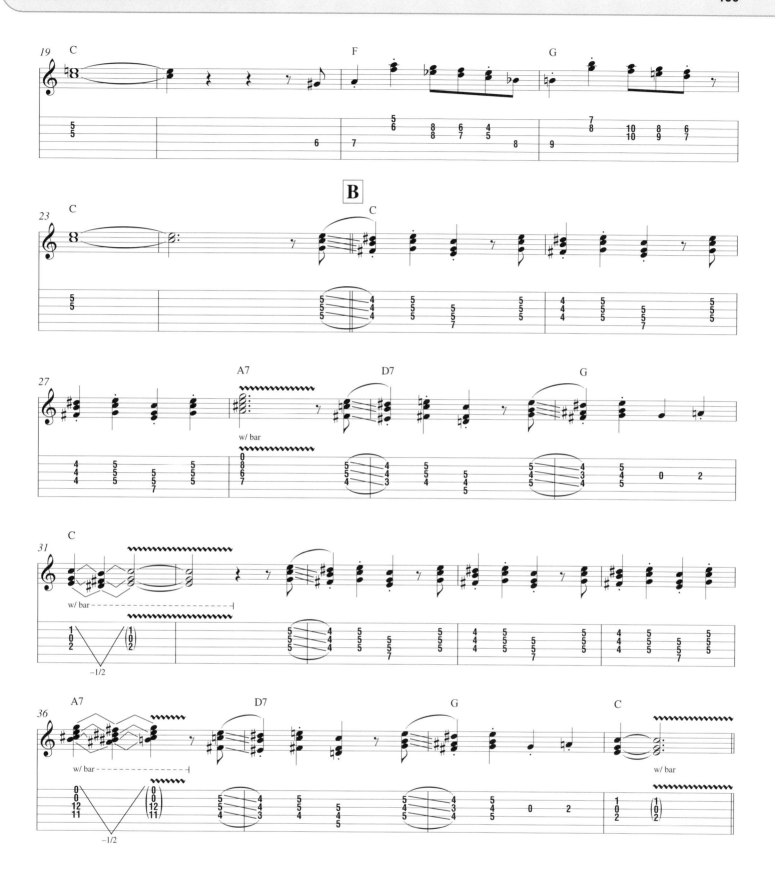

# ESSENTIAL TECHNIQUES

We don't always think about "technique" when studying guitar heroes, because so many of these heroes have built their work around soloing on the guitar, which often entails a lot of time learning licks, integrating them into their repertoire, and learning how to put those licks together in new ways. Of course, learning scale patterns and fingerings falls under the "technique" balloon, so nearly every guitarist spends *some* time working on technique before discovering how to apply those patterns to soloing along with their licks. But we often focus on the *licks*, without a lot of thought for the technical side of things.

Chet Atkins is a bit of an anomaly in this realm, because much of his playing was actually closely tied to the underlying techniques that he applied to the guitar. He certainly knew plenty of scale patterns and even licks, but it's really techniques like alternate-bass fingerpicking, cascading harmonic runs (often called *harp harmonics*), and a variety of rolls and picking patterns that brought these scales and licks to life. In this section, we'll explore the foundation of Atkins' playing by looking at the essential techniques he used to create his unique sound.

## The Alternating Bass

*Alternate-bass fingerpicking* is the foundation of what most people think of when they hear Chet Atkins. You literally "alternate" between bass strings with your thumb, which acts as an independent "boom-chuck" backup while your fingers apply melody and harmony on the top strings. Today it's one of the more common types of acoustic fingerpicking, for both solo fingerpickers and those who accompany themselves singing songs. But this wasn't the case back when Atkins got started on guitar. In fact, he was a huge factor in popularizing the style—a style sometimes referred to as "Travis picking" because of the huge influence Merle Travis had in popularizing the technique before Chet did. Travis himself was inspired by two guitarists he knew—Mose Rager and Ike Everly (the father of the Everly Brothers). As Travis's son Thom Bresh described it, he'd watch Rager using a version of the technique while picking at the "company store." Travis started using the technique in his own way, and he'd use his thumb to play the low strings on beats 1 and 3 of the measure and play the higher strings on beats 2 and 4. If we were playing an E chord, for example, this is how it might sound:

Techniques
Example 1

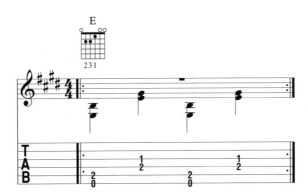

Now, for the most part, Travis pretty much stuck to this type of pattern, where he's aiming for the same strings in the bass part each time. He'd also almost always hit multiple strings with his thumb, sometimes strumming pretty much all the way through, like this:

Techniques
Example 2

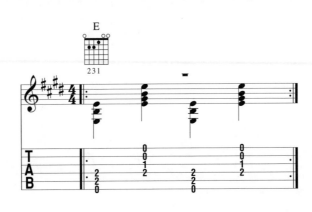

Chet, on the other hand, was much more precise about which strings he hit, so if he was playing the same E chord, the thumb part would often sound more like this:

**Techniques Example 3**

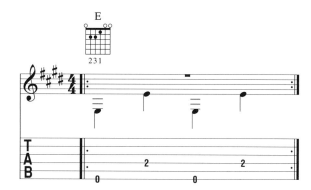

Of course, Atkins would sometimes hit several strings at once, but it was still much more of a precision pick than the wide brushes that Travis did. Here's an example:

**Techniques Example 4**

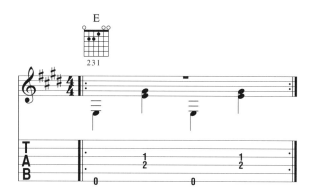

Aside from this, another main difference between Atkins' style and Travis's is that Atkins would often *alternate* a set of bass notes. For instance, he might alternate the lower sixth string with a fifth-string bass note. So, for our E chord, we'd be playing the sixth string on beat 1 and fifth string on beat 3:

**Techniques Example 5**

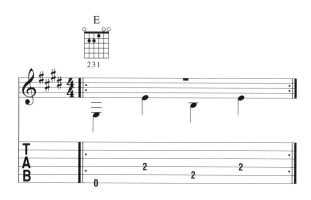

While our previous patterns alternated between the lower and higher string sets, this is perhaps more precisely the "alternating" that "alternate-bass" fingerpicking refers to. Of course, this could manifest itself in many different ways. For instance, if you're playing an A chord up the neck and fretting the bass note with your thumb (which we'll explore more in depth later in this chapter), you could alternate the bass by removing your thumb from the string, like this:

**Techniques Example 6**

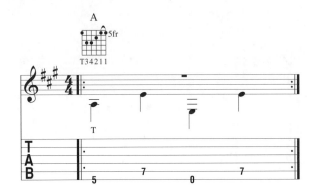

You could also alternate from a higher string to a lower one. For instance, this four-string A7 shape up the neck alternates between the open fifth and sixth strings, in reverse order of the E chord we previously looked at:

**Techniques Example 7**

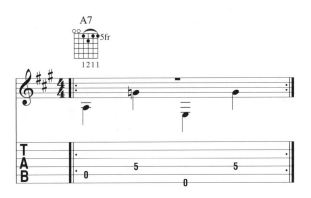

## Palm Muting

Another key aspect of Chet's signature alternate-bass fingerpicking is *palm muting*, a technique where you rest the palm of your picking hand gently up against the strings near the bridge to mute them. Use the fleshy part of the outside of your palm to do this, gently touching just the bottom three strings to mute notes that you pluck with your thumb. Here's how that looks on the strings:

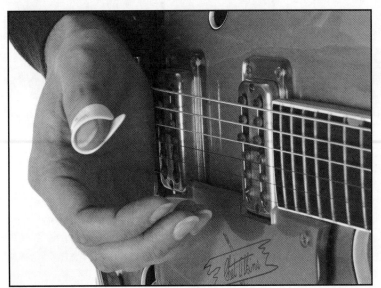

With your palm comfortably muting the strings, you'll hear a noticeable difference when playing that alternating bass pattern with an E chord. There's a fairly wide variation on how much you can mute the strings, and Atkins would mute them quite heavily—but not so much that you couldn't hear the notes anymore. If you're applying too much pressure, or you're muting too far in front of the bridge, you'll only hear a percussive "plunk." If that's the case, let off just enough pressure (or move back a bit) so that you can hear the note thumping out and quickly decaying, as demonstrated in the following example.

Techniques
Example 8

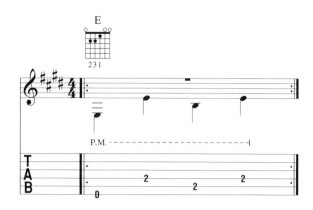

If you haven't done it much before, it may take you a little while to get comfortable with this concept. You can practice it on your own by applying it to chord progressions you already play. Here's an E–A–B7–E progression to get you started:

Techniques
Example 9

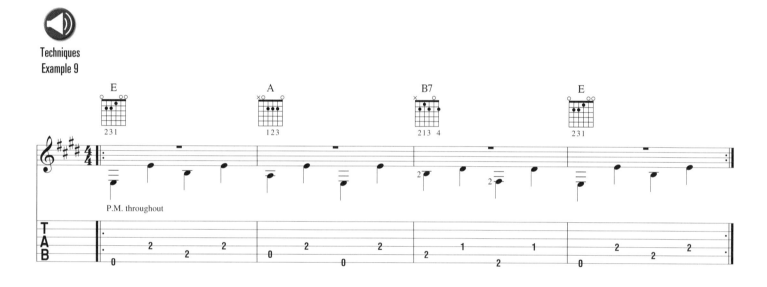

As you fret the B7 shape, you'll have to move the middle finger of your fretting hand down to the sixth string to grab the alternate-bass note (F♯) down there. Moving the bottom finger down a string to grab an alternate-bass note like this is a common practice in Atkins' playing (and alternate-bass fingerpicking, as well).

We've written out the "P.M." marking that designates palm muting in the previous examples, but this happens in virtually every Chet Atkins song, so any time there's alternate bass, this is implied (and not always written).

## Melody Against the Bass

Here's where things get interesting. Atkins keeps that thumb plunking away steadily underneath while adding melody notes on top with his fingers. If you're new to this style, it can help to start in an open tuning, where many of the bass notes (and melody notes) can be open strings, making things easier on the fretting hand. Here's a basic melody in G over an alternate-bass pattern in open G tuning (D–G–D–G–B–D). This is a barebones example, but it's a good one with which to start:

Techniques
Example 10

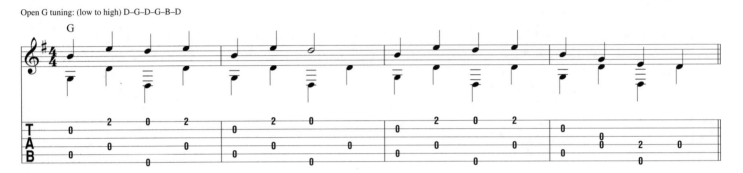

Check out how the melody on the final beat goes down and "merges" with the bass line. This happens quite often in Atkins' music and, when it does, he simply plays it with his thumb, which helps keep everything in rhythm because he's not dropping that propulsive thumb groove. Sometimes notes are written doubled up like this to show that it's the melody note but played in the bass; most often, though, that note is only written once (either with stems pointing down to indicate it's played by the thumb, or with stems pointing up along with a "p" between notation and tablature to indicate that the thumb plays it even though it's part of the melody). Now this last example sounds pretty basic, and much of that is due to the melody notes falling on the beat along with the bass notes. Atkins made his lines interesting by *syncopating* melody notes (accenting the offbeat by having them fall between the beats). If those melody notes fall between the beats, you can see that our whole pattern picks up a lot more steam:

Techniques
Example 11

Open G tuning: (low to high) D–G–D–G–B–D

On top of this, he'd use hammer-ons and pull-offs to enable him to pluck notes on the beat and still have a note following in the syncopated offbeat. Likewise, he could pick a syncopated note and hammer or pull off that note to grab another melody note on the beat. Here's how Atkins himself played the opening measures of "Black Mountain Rag." You'll see that he shifted the first note down to the third string. This allows him to hammer-on from a pickup note a half step below (which is actually a melody note that we left out in the previous examples to make it easier). Also note how he plays the melody completely with the thumb in the fourth measure—another technique that pops up in his songs quite a bit in short spurts. This happens especially when the melody easily falls on the beat and is accessible on the lower strings.

Techniques
Example 12

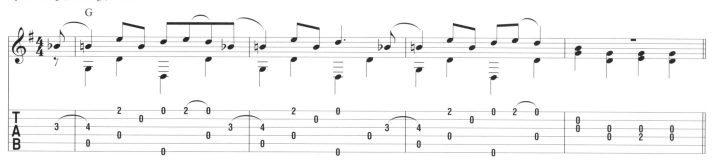

Open G tuning: (low to high) D–G–D–G–B–D

## Former *Frets* Editor Mark Hanson on Chet Atkins

"For many years Chet and his associate John Knowles produced monthly columns for *Guitar Player* and *Frets* magazines," says Hanson. "As an editor at *Frets*, it was my privilege to work with these kind, immensely talented, and punctual(!) people."

Along with Atkins' talent as a player and instructor, Hanson notes that "Chet was very aware of trends in the music industry—evidenced notably by his 1966 LP *Chet Picks on the Beatles*, his covers of pop hits like 'Snowbird' and 'Both Sides Now,' and his work with Dire Straits' Mark Knopfler."

And while Atkins considered himself a guitarist first and foremost, Hanson posits, "As brilliant, innovative, creative, and hard-working as Chet Atkins was as a guitarist, inspiring legions of followers over many decades, he may have made a larger impact on society as a record producer. He was the brain behind making what many considered 'hillbilly' music of the Appalachians more palatable to the masses, setting the stage for the behemoth that the country music industry has become today."

# Thumb Fretting

Atkins often wrapped his thumb over the neck to fret notes on the bass strings. Here's how that looks when playing a G major barre chord at the third fret:

While classical enthusiasts might frown at this type of technique (or even become physically ill!) because your thumb is no longer planted on the neck and providing pressure and a pivot point to quickly navigate around, there are actually several great reasons to use this technique. (Though if it hurts your hands or they're too small to fret over the neck, don't push it! You don't want to risk hurting your fingers or bringing on tendonitis.) One of the best reasons is that a standard major barre chord like the G chord we just played would use *all* of your fingers just to play that one chord. By using your thumb to fret the low bass note, however, we free up some of your fingers to play melody notes on top. While the adjacent image shows us using all of our fingers for the thumb-fretted version, we don't really need all those notes to play the chord. We can leave out the note on the fifth string, for example, and move that ring finger up to the fourth string. Of course, we'll have to remember to only alternate between the sixth and fourth strings for this shape, since that fifth string is muted.

So, for instance, a melody like this would be impossible to play using a standard barre chord fretted entirely by the fingers. But when we fret with our thumb, it's no problem:

Techniques
Example 13

Another reason to fret with your thumb is that you can access notes *behind* the barre, like the following example, which—again—would be impossible to play with a standard barre. For those second-fret F♯ notes, just reach back with your index finger:

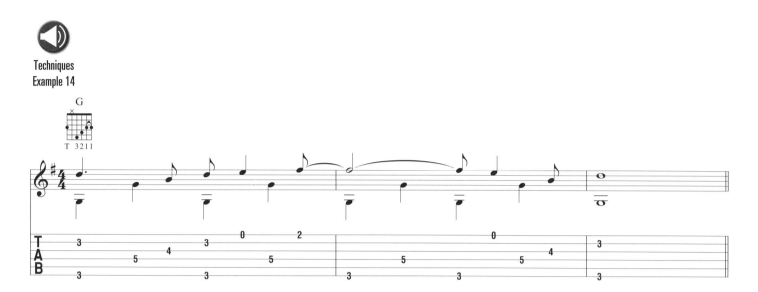

Techniques
Example 14

## Thumb-Fretting Two Strings

Yes, it might sound crazy at first, but Atkins (and Merle Travis) would sometimes fret *two* strings with his thumb. Here's how that looks on a D9 chord at the fourth fret:

This may prove a little too difficult for quite a few people—especially if your hands are on the smaller side. If you find this technique unattainable, you can often adapt your playing to still get the same (or nearly the same) effect. For instance, this picked D9 chord example could be fretted entirely with the thumb, but you could also use a standard fingering, with your middle finger rocking between the fifth- and sixth-string bass notes. Atkins himself would sometimes do this and, for this particular line, it will sound exactly the same.

Techniques
Example 15

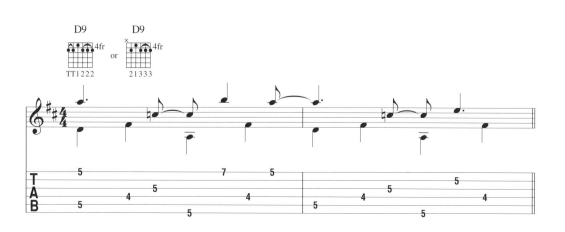

There are some instances, however, where he uses all four fingers to fret notes on the higher strings, like on this chord shape, which he uses in "Mister Sandman." To play this without thumb fretting, you'd have to leave out a note or two:

The Vibrato Bar

While the vibrato bar has often become affiliated with the shredding days of the 1980s, especially in conjunction with the Floyd Rose tremolo system, much earlier guitars like the Gretsch Country Gentleman (that Atkins helped design) were often equipped with a Bigsby bar. Atkins and others took great advantage of it to shape their sound.

## Vibrato

As you'd expect from a "vibrato" bar, this metal arm was used by Atkins to add a fluttery vibrato to notes and chords—especially those that were held out for a few beats. He'd position his hand over the bar, often resting the last knuckle of his pinky against the guitar when using just the thumbpick or planting the tip of that pinky against the top of the guitar—in both cases with the bar handily tucked right underneath so that he could curl his hand inward to grab it in one quick motion:

*Position when picking single notes or chords with thumbpick.*

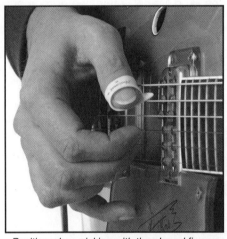

*Position when picking with thumb and fingers.*

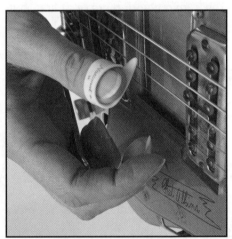

*Position when performing vibrato.*

*Vibrato* happens when a note moves subtly up and down around the target pitch, but in this type of vibrato, it's mostly moved *up* and released back. To do this, gently pull the bar away from the guitar and then move it back to its original position repeatedly. Here's how that sounds applied to a chord:

Techniques
Example 16

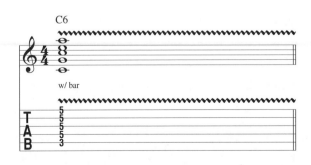

## Dips

Along with vibrato, Atkins often used the bar for *dips* (or "dives") to help color his chords. To play a dip, pluck a note or chord, push down lightly on the bar to lower the pitch, and let off the pressure so that the bar releases to its normal state. Here's how that sounds when applied to a chord. Here, we dip a half step lower then the original chord. While you can go further than this, it's the distance most favored by Chet:

Techniques
Example 17

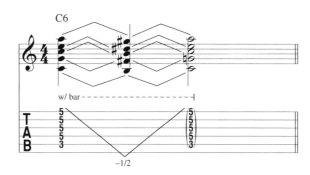

You can perform a dip one of two ways. If you have a little bit of time, you can grab the bar just like you did for the vibrato and use the grip of your hand to push down and let go of the bar. But when Atkins wanted to add a quick dip right after his hand had just been picking, he'd leave his palm open and just push down quickly with an open palm.

# *Picking Techniques*

A huge part of Atkins' playing revolves around his pick-hand technique. In fact, even the alternate-bass fingerpicking falls into this category (but that is a large enough topic on its own that it received its own section). Here, we'll look at the picking techniques he used to create melodies whenever he wasn't playing the alternate bass.

## Thumb-Only Lead Lines

There are plenty of guitar heroes who played single-note lines much more often than Chet Atkins, but he certainly played his own share, as well. We often affiliate single-note playing with a flatpick—one held between your thumb and index finger—but Atkins played with a thumbpick. The thumbpick gave him more power while also enabling him to be more precise with his alternate-bass picking, but it also happens to be more difficult to play single-note lines with precision when using a thumbpick, because it's much more comfortable to play downstrokes with a thumbpick than it is to play upstrokes. A flatpick, on the other hand, allows you to play upstrokes as well. So Atkins would get around this problem by holding his index finger up against his thumb, essentially creating a "virtual flatpick" with his thumbpick. This gave him much more control over his upstrokes.

Try the following line out using your thumbpick as a virtual pick by holding your index finger and thumb together.

Techniques
Example 18

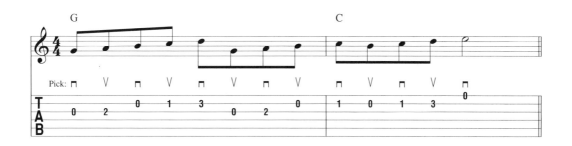

## Thumb-Index Lead Lines

Chet would also play single-note lines by alternating with his thumb and index finger, using his thumb for the downstrokes and his index finger for the upstrokes. Try this out over the same line we just played with a "virtual pick."

Techniques
Example 19

This type of picking also comes in handy whenever you have string skips—and especially when alternating between lower and higher strings—like in this line:

Techniques
Example 20

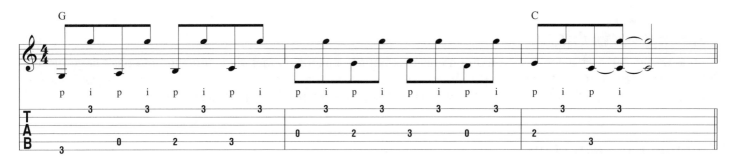

Try the previous line out with the "virtual pick" method to see how much easier it is when you play it by alternating between your thumb and index finger.

## Rolls

Playing banjo-type rolls on the guitar was one of Chet Atkins' favorite tricks. In fact, it's a broad enough topic that we'll only scratch the surface in this section, but you'll find more specific rolls and tricks in the other sections of this book. Basic banjo roll patterns involve your thumb and two fingers to play three strings in a row. Here's the most common roll pattern, often referred to as the *forward roll*:

Techniques
Example 21

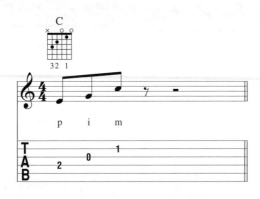

Of course, the roll sounds best when it's repeated, and that's exactly what we do here. But since it's three notes long, and we often play in 4/4 time, it takes *three whole measures* to cycle all the way through when we adapt this roll to the guitar. (On the banjo, that's not always the case, since the lowest string is the *highest pitched* string and is sometimes not played first in this pattern.)

Techniques
Example 22

To keep the neat roll quality while also wedging it into a common 4/4 time signature, people often cut the roll short at the end of the second measure, holding out the middle-finger pluck on the "and" of beat 2 throughout the rest of the measure:

Techniques
Example 23

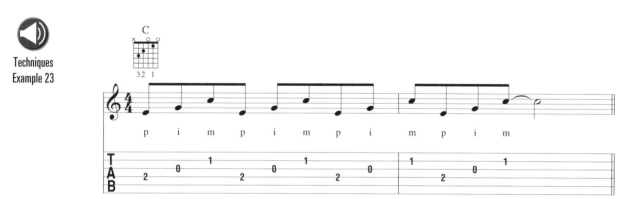

As you might expect, there are many other types of rolls you can play. For instance, you could reverse the pattern, playing m–i–p throughout:

Techniques
Example 24

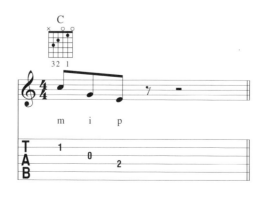

Or you could put those two together for a forward/reverse pattern like this:

Techniques
Example 25

p    i    m    p    m    i    p    m

We'll explore other types throughout the other sections of this book, and you can certainly explore your own rolls. There are many great ones out there to discover!

# Harmonics

The bell-like chime created by harmonics is a distinctive sound on the guitar and one that Chet Atkins used in his playing for some unique effects. To get a handle on Chet's harmonic use, we must first look at *natural harmonics*—the harmonics that naturally occur in relation to the open strings. Then, we'll look at *artificial harmonics* (including *harp harmonics)*, which are those that are generated via fretted notes. These artificial harmonics are the tool that Atkins used to create cascading harmonic runs and chordal harmonics—two concepts explored later in the "Stylistic DNA" section.

## Natural Harmonics

Natural harmonics are created when you lightly touch a specific place on the string while plucking it. These places on the string, called *nodes*, are where the wave comes together (or the place where the wave crosses the string, if you were able to see the wave as it vibrates). There are many nodes where you can create harmonics, and they get closer together as you approach the nut of your guitar, but the most common places to play harmonics are on the 12th, seventh, and fifth frets. Try this out on the first string of your guitar by lightly touching the string at the 12th fret, *directly over the fret* (not behind the fret, as you would when fretting a note):

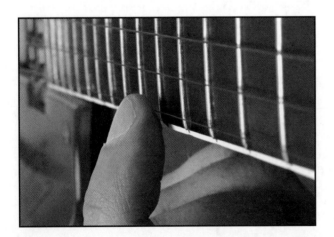

Don't apply pressure to the string; simply touch it, pluck the string with your picking hand, and release your fret-hand finger from the string just after the note sounds (holding the finger in place can dampen the sound). You'll have to practice the timing of this move until you find the optimum motion of plucking and releasing the fret-hand finger. Here's how it sounds:

Techniques
Example 26

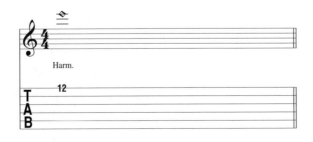

Harm.

12

Once you can get a clear sound, try the harmonics at the seventh and fifth frets:

Techniques
Example 27

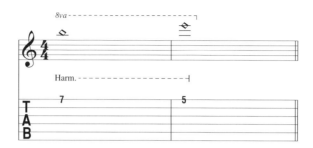

You can play more than one harmonic simultaneously on the same string by laying your fret-hand finger lightly across two or more strings. Here's how that looks playing harmonics on all six strings:

Try this out in the following example, which first demonstrates harmonics in string pairs and then across all six strings:

Techniques
Example 28

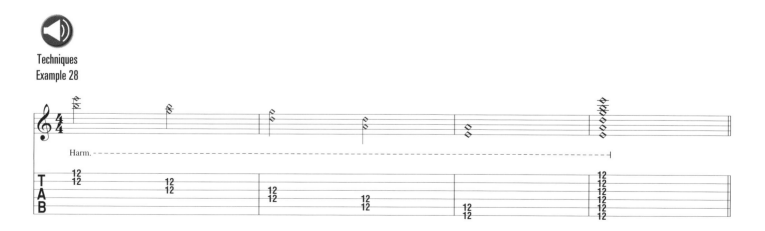

## Artificial (Harp) Harmonics

To produce artificial harmonics, you create your own node by fretting a note with your fretting hand. This essentially takes the place of the nut, and you can then create a harmonic in relation to that fretted note by lightly touching the string higher than that and plucking it. Because you're using your fretting hand to hold down a fret, you'll have to use your *picking hand* to lightly touch the string *and* to pluck the note. Use your index finger to lightly touch the note and pluck the string behind the index finger (closer to the bridge) with your thumb. (You can use your middle or ring finger to touch the string, too. But most people start with the index finger.) Again, it's most common to touch the string either 12, seven, or five frets above that fretted note. Here's an artificial harmonic produced by fretting the first fret and lightly touching the node 12 frets above that (at the 13th fret):

Techniques
Example 29

As you can see in the tablature, both fret numbers are shown, with the higher pick-hand number shown to the right in parentheses. Occasionally, a footnote may describe the technique and one or the other of the pair of fret numbers will be left out. (In these cases, the note will usually detail which one that is and whether you need to touch the string 12 frets above or fret the string 12 frets below.)

The beauty of artificial harmonics is that you can play harmonics for any note you want, which enables you to play single-note melodies just as you would with standard notes. Simply play the melody and lightly touch and pluck 12 frets above, like this:

Techniques
Example 30

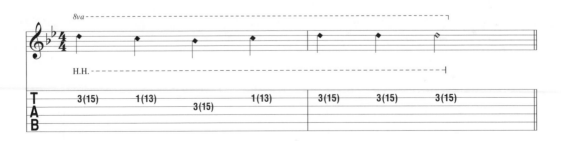

Chet used artificial harmonics in a unique way by integrating them into shapes and alternating with non-harmonic notes to create cascading harmonic sounds. He also used them along with fretted notes to play dyads and three- or four-note chords. We'll explore these more closely in the following "Stylistic DNA" section.

# STYLISTIC DNA

Here we'll take a look at what goes on behind Chet's playing by looking at the specific way he approached the guitar with his unique techniques—particularly roll patterns and harmonics. When you understand how he approaches the instrument along with the thought behind it, this shines a light on his stylistic DNA and allows you to use the same processes to play the same things or come up with your own ideas by using the same philosophy.

## Chet's Approach to Rolls and Roll Patterns

Atkins came up with what seemed like a limitless supply of roll patterns to create his melodies and licks, but they all really distill down to just several primary building blocks. First, he was very fond of the forward roll, a repeating thumb-index-middle picking pattern adapted from the banjo that we've looked at in other sections of this book:

DNA
Example 1

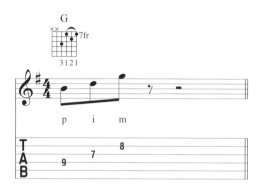

One of his favorite ways to use this roll was to play a pattern that alternated the middle finger between the second and first strings, like this:

DNA
Example 2

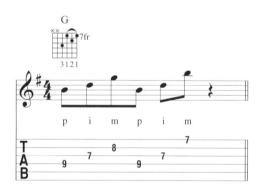

When you use the open first string, as Chet often did, this pattern creates a bit more of a "cascading" sound with shapes up the neck, like our previous G chord. This is especially true when you play a longer pattern, like this two-measure one:

DNA
Example 3

Atkins used this particular roll pattern all over the place and played it for complete song melodies, including "Cascade" and "Dizzy Strings." In fact, these two tunes even use the roll within the very same context—an eight-measure chord progression that changes chords every two bars (with the exception of the sixth and seventh measures, which both have one-measure chord changes). "Cascade" uses a I–II–IV–V–I progression in the key of C, while "Dizzy Strings" uses a I–IV–ii–V–I progression in the key of G. Let's try the same thing in the key of D to see how this approach works over a progression like this. Here, let's use a similar progression—a I–II–ii–V–I (D–E–Em–A–D). Let's embellish these shapes to create D9–Eadd9–Em9–A13–D9 harmonies and apply our roll:

DNA
Example 4

Notice how the shapes have notes that are close to that open E string, but that E notes, especially in the same octave, have been avoided in the shapes themselves, so as not to duplicate that open string. This creates a more lush sounding passage.

Another roll pattern that Atkins favored is the reverse roll, which he often started with the thumb, like this:

DNA
Example 5

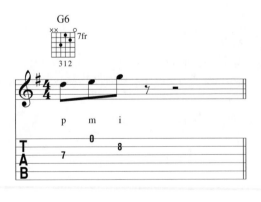

Add two more small, partial roll patterns—the thumb-index and thumb-middle—and you have all the building blocks to create most of what Chet played when it comes to rolls:

**DNA**
**Example 6**

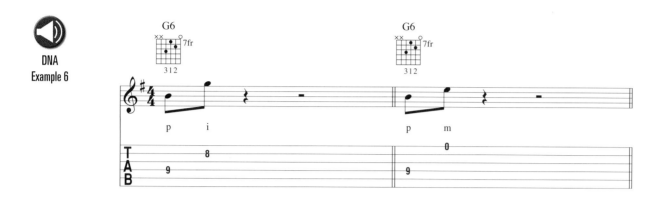

So, to recap, here are the four roll parts:

**DNA**
**Example 7**

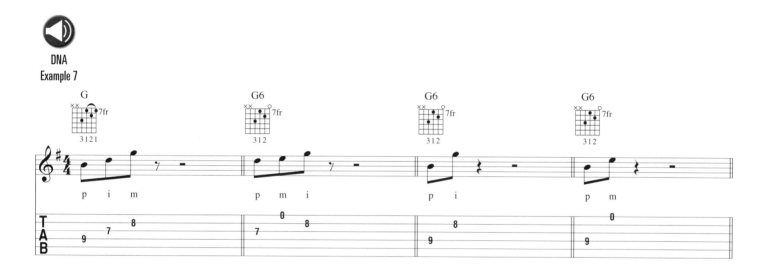

He'd combine these in quite a few different ways. For instance, here's another of his favorite extended roll patterns that incorporates the reverse roll:

**DNA**
**Example 8**

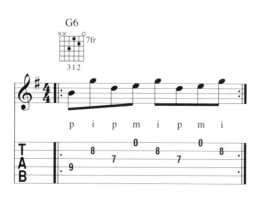

Along with these patterns themselves, Atkins would also experiment with the strings he was picking. So, for instance, our previous combined pattern could have ended up like this, too:

DNA
Example 9

# Chet's Approach to Cascading Harp Harmonics

Chet created his immediately recognizable cascading harp harmonic runs by approaching the concept from several distinct ways, though they may *sound* very similar. The first method revolves around using a six-string barre with the index finger, which he'd use as-is or manipulate it by adding a finger here and there to better match the underlying harmony. The second method revolves around following the chord changes with usually smaller chord shapes that match the underlying harmony and applying the cascading technique along with pull-offs or hammer-ons to create a line or lick.

## The Full-Barre Concept

Though the technique involved with mixing artificial harmonics and standard notes is difficult, the idea behind this is deceptively simple: a basic one-finger barre across all six strings. The deceptive part here is that when you actually *play* a barre across all six strings, it doesn't sound particularly pleasing. For instance, when you do this at the fifth fret, you get this muddy-sounding Am11 chord.

DNA
Example 10

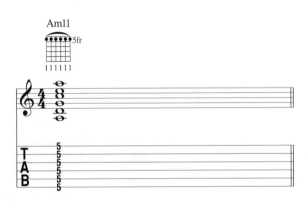

But when you add Atkins' harp-style artificial harmonics to this barre, you get a very different sound. To do this, you alternate between a standard note and an artificial harmonic two strings lower. Starting on the fourth string with a standard note and then alternating as you go up the strings gives us this line, which is often how Chet played it. As you can see, the melody now spells out the notes of a C major pentatonic scale (C–D–E–G–A), which would sound great over a C chord:

DNA
Example 11

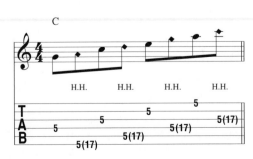

Of course, that line would work fine over an Am chord, as well, since those notes also spell out an A minor pentatonic scale (A–C–D–E–G). Chet would do this, too, but he might also manipulate the place he started and ended on, to highlight the A note more prominently:

DNA
Example 12

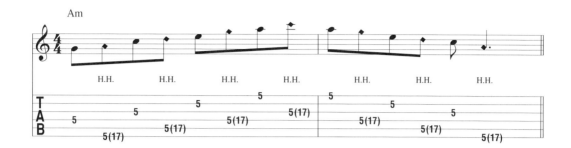

But it doesn't end there. Atkins realized that by simply adding a finger or two, you could make the line sound great over other chords, as well. For instance, by just placing your index finger on the sixth fret of the second string, you *now* spell out all the notes of the F major pentatonic scale, so this line and its variants would work well over an F or Dm chord:

DNA
Example 13

Finally, Atkins would fill in more notes in a run by playing pull-offs on the standard notes. Here's how he'd apply that to create a fuller C major scale run going down and up the strings. Notice how the added pull-offs affect your picking hand. Any time you have a pull-off, you'll be playing a *three-note* pattern, because the pull-off inserts an extra eighth note into the thumb-index pattern. So remember to pause with your thumb while you play the pull-off, or else you'll have a cascading accident on the fretboard!

DNA
Example 14

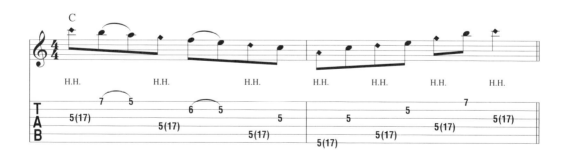

Several things stand out from this example: 1) Atkins pretty much exclusively used pull-offs to access extra notes—never hammer-ons, 2) Atkins always played these pull-offs on the higher strings with the standard notes only, and 3) He *only* played those pull-offs on runs and parts of runs that were *descending*. Perhaps this happened because the run would sound less scalar if he added a hammer-on, since he'd be *ascending* the scale, and since he never really played hammer-ons within these runs, that eliminated those extra notes from his ascending lines.

## The Chordal Concept

Another key approach Chet used to create harp harmonics was to start with chord shapes that correspond to the underlying harmony and then use some of the same techniques he used for the barre method to come up with cascading lines. For instance, if he were playing over a D7–G7–E7–Amaj7 chord progression in the key of A, he might start out with these four-note drop-two voicings on the top four strings:

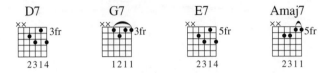

As shown above, he'd sometimes use the same exact harmony of the underlying chords (for the D7 and G7 chords), but he'd also add extra color via adding extensions (like on the G7 and Amaj7 chords). He then would apply the harp technique to get a line like this:

**DNA**
**Example 15**

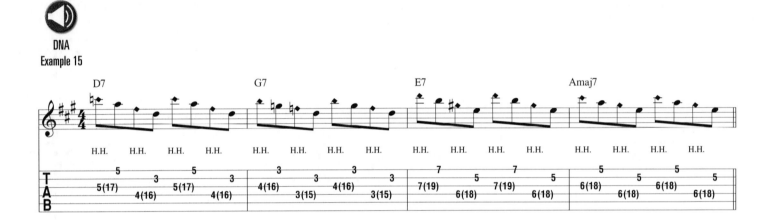

But he would also add pull-offs, as before, to create an even more fluid line, like this:

**DNA**
**Example 16**

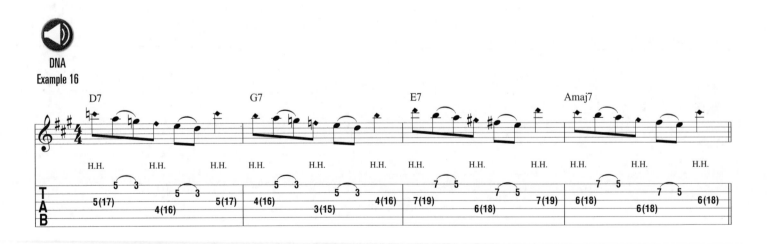

He would either pull-off from a chord tone to a barred or fretted note below, or he would add a note above a chord tone and pull-off to that chord tone. As you can see, this creates a similar line to the previous method, but instead of approaching it from a straight barre and adding notes, here he approached it by visualizing chords based around the underlying progression.

## Chet's Approach to Dyads and Chords with Artificial Harmonics

Atkins was also fond of using harmonics within a dyad or chord in a similar manner to how he used harmonics in cascading runs. When playing dyads, he was particularly fond of these 6th shapes on the top four strings:

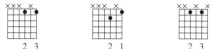

One of the reasons for this is that the lower note, which he would always play as a harmonic, would pop an octave up—higher than the other note—inverting the interval to a 3rd, which makes a great sound for harmonized melodies. It's shown here with the first notes of "Mary Had a Little Lamb":

**DNA Example 17**

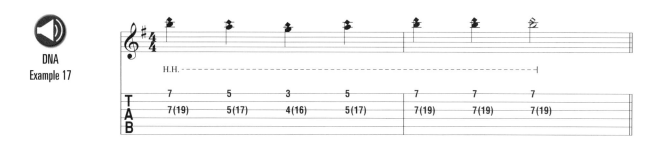

Of course, he would fill in melodies with plenty of other intervals, as well, but these 6ths were often the foundation from which he began. For example, 3rds or 4ths, like these, would be integrated into the line, but often as a result of the melody.

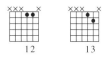

For instance, he might take a melody like the following and start with 6ths but add in the other intervals—or even a single note here or there—to harmonize the whole melody:

**DNA Example 18**

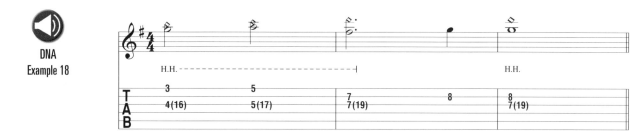

For chordal harmonics, Atkins would again almost exclusively play the *lowest* note in a chord as a harmonic, fretting the higher two notes normally (it was rarely, if ever, *more* than a three-note chord). He favored shapes on three consecutive strings, like these major and minor shapes:

Major Shapes                                                                                                                                     Minor Shapes

Notice how here he goes all the way down to shapes on the bottom three strings, because having a harmonic on the lowest string makes the chord sound less muddy since that note moves up an octave. In the context of a triad (as opposed to intervals), moving the harmonic note up an octave simply puts the chord in a higher inversion. So a root-position C chord turns into a first-inversion C chord, while a second-inversion C chord turns into a root position C:

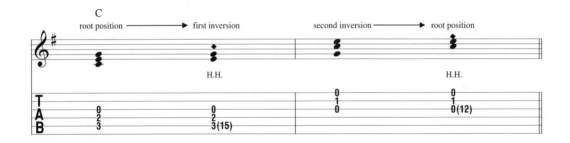

Atkins would use these to harmonize a song in chord-melody style, usually moving from chord to chord (or inversion to inversion) for each melody note, but occasionally altering one note, like the harmonic, to create a different melody note over the same harmony. Check it out here on the opening of Brahms's "Lullaby":

DNA
Example 19

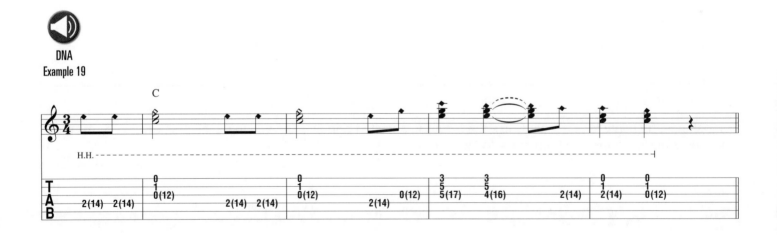

A great example of Chet's use of harmonics in chords can be found in his recording of "When You Wish upon a Star."

## Three-Notes-Per-String Scale Runs

Chet often created scale runs using open strings against fretted notes up the neck, which we've studied extensively in the "Licks" section of this book. But when he *did* play closed-position scale shapes up the neck (which he also did quite a bit of), he was especially fond of three-notes-per string scale patterns. Perhaps one of the reasons Chet liked these types of patterns so much is that they enabled him to use each of his most favored pick-hand fingers—the thumb, index, and middle—in a consistent pattern across the strings. For a descending pattern, he would often use a thumb-middle-index pattern to run down a scale:

DNA
Example 20

Descending G Major Scale

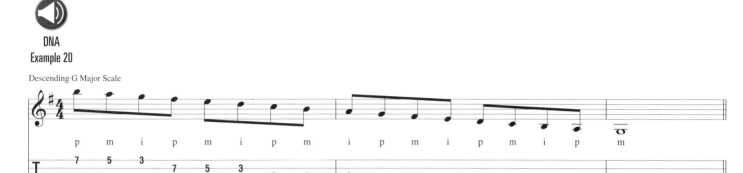

But the pick-hand fingering would also depend on where he started within each pattern. For instance, this ascending Mixolydian run was one of his favorites, and he'd use a middle-index-thumb (m-i-p) pattern on each string. Since the root note falls on the *second* of the three-notes-per-string pattern on the bottom string, he'd start on the second note of the pattern—with his index finger, like this:

DNA
Example 21

Ascending G Mixolydian Mode

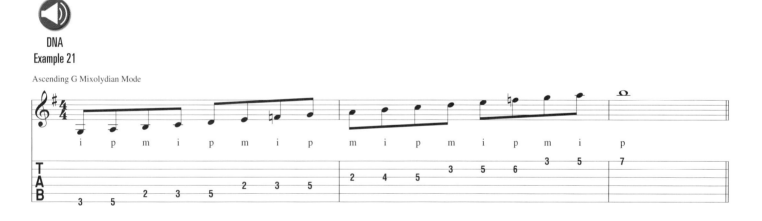

And Chet was also likely to play an ascending major-scale pattern in the same place as the previous Mixolydian scale, which only alters a few notes:

DNA
Example 22

Ascending G Major Scale

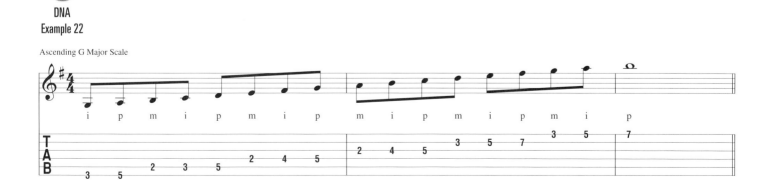

Another pattern that Chet was likely to play is a major pattern with the root on the fifth string, here shown as a C major scale:

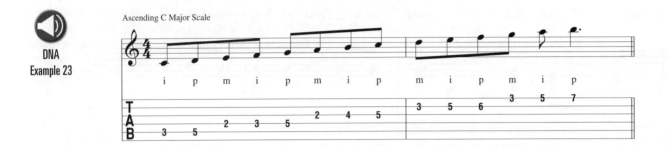

DNA
Example 23

Since these are all closed-position shapes, Atkins used them in many different keys/positions.

## Approaching Notes and Chords from a Half Step Below

Chet was adept at using half-step approach tones and chords to create a strong resolution or to create a discordant tension and then release it. He often did this via the more common method of simply sliding a note or shape up the fretboard, but one of the most distinctive ways he did this was with the vibrato bar.

Here's how he'd aid the resolution to a note or chord by sliding up into it, resolving on the beat (or on the strong beat, as in the second full measure). Every chord below is resolved this way, along with the opening single-note line F#–G:

DNA
Example 24

Sometimes he'd use this trick to embellish a chord shape by first playing the shape, sliding down to the half step below, and then coming back for resolution:

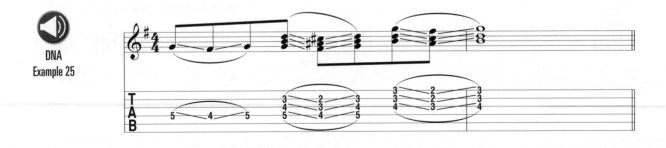

DNA
Example 25

To create extra tension, he'd occasionally play the discordant notes or chords on the strong beats, which creates an even stronger moment of discord, before then resolving to the chord a half step above, as shown in this excerpted line from "Down Hill Drag":

DNA
Example 26

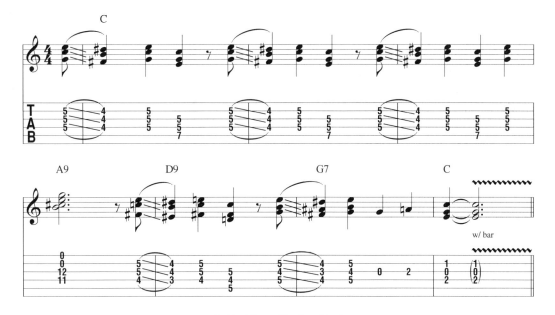

When using his vibrato bar, Atkins would dip into the chord a half step below and then let up on the bar to return.

DNA
Example 27

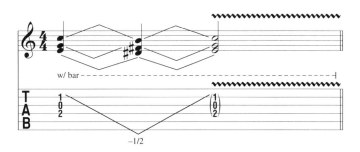

Some of his most unique sounds with this concept come from pre-dives on the vibrato bar. Atkins had that half-step dive programmed into his muscle memory so well that he could effortlessly play lines with half-step pre-dives. Here, he cleanly bent the strings down a half step with the bar before striking the strings so that the note or chord a half step below would sound (relative to what he was fretting). Then all he'd have to do is release the bar for the chord to resolve up into his fretted note or chord.

DNA
Example 28

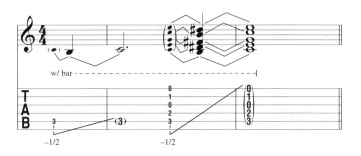

This technique plays a prominent role in the main theme of "Trambone."

# MUST HEAR

Chet Atkins left a huge legacy on record, and since it started back in the 1950s, some of his original releases are hard to come by. Because of this, we'll also list essential compilations at the end, so that any tracks that are hard to come by via their original release can be easily accessed.

## Original LP/EP Releases

### Stringin' Along with Chet Atkins (12" LP Release), 1955

**Essential Tracks**
Galloping on the Guitar
Black Mountain Rag
Oh by Jingo!

### Finger Style Guitar, 1956

**Essential Tracks**
Swedish Rhapsody
Liza
Unchained Melody

### Mister Guitar, 1959

**Essential Tracks**
Country Gentleman
Rainbow
Jessie

### Christmas with Chet Atkins, 1961

**Essential Tracks**
White Christmas
Silver Bells
Jingle Bell Rock

### Guitar Country, 1964

**Essential Tracks**
Freight Train
Nine Pound Hammer
Vaya Con Dios

### More of That Guitar Country, 1965

**Essential Tracks**
Yakety Axe
Old Joe Clark
Blowin' in the Wind

### Chet Atkins Picks on the Beatles, 1966

**Essential Tracks**
Yesterday
I Feel Fine

### Me & Jerry, 1970 (with Jerry Reed)

**Essential Tracks**
Cannon Ball Rag
Stump Water
Tennessee Stud
Something

### Me & Chet, 1971 (Jerry Reed with Chet)

**Essential Tracks**
Jerry's Breakdown
Limehouse Blues
Mystery Train

### Me and My Guitar, 1977

**Essential Tracks**
Cascade
Struttin'

### Chester and Lester, 1977 (with Les Paul)

**Essential Tracks**
Avalon
Caravan
It Had to Be You

## *Reflections*, 1980 (with Doc Watson)

**Essential Tracks**
Dill Pickle Rag
Tennessee Rag/Beaumont Rag
Black and White/Ragtime Annie

## *Country After All These Years*, 1981

**Essential Tracks**
Orange Blossom Special
Wildwood Flower

## *Stay Tuned*, 1985 (with Various Artists)

**Essential Tracks**
Sunrise (with George Benson)
Please Stay Tuned
Cosmic Square Dance (with Mark Knopfler)

## *Neck and Neck*, 1990 (with Mark Knopfler)

**Essential Tracks**
Poor Boy Blues
I'll See You in My Dreams
There'll Be Some Changes Made

## *Almost Alone*, 1996

**Essential Tracks**
Big Foot
Ave Maria
Jam Man

## *The Day Finger Pickers Took over the World*, 1997 (with Tommy Emmanuel)

**Essential Tracks**
Road to Gundaghi/Waltzing Matilda
Dixie McGuire
Tip Toe Through the Bluegrass

# *Compilations*

## *Guitar Legend: The RCA Years*, 2000

**Essential Tracks**
Black Mountain Rag
Blue Angel
Cascade
Chinatown, My Chinatown
Country Gentleman
Dizzy Strings
Down Hill Drag
Galloping on the Guitar
Mountain Melody
Mister Sandman
Trambone
Windy and Warm
Yakety Axe

## *RCA Country Legends*, 2001

**Essential Tracks**
Barber Shop Rag
Boo Boo Stick Beat
Liza
Tiger Rag
Twichy

## *The Essential Chet Atkins: The Columbia Years*, 2004

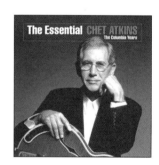

**Essential Tracks**
Cosmic Square Dance
Dixie McGuire
I'll See You in My Dreams
Imagine
Jam Man
Poor Boy Blues
Road to Gundaghi/Waltzing Matilda
Sneakin' Around

## *The Essential Chet Atkins*, 2007

**Essential Tracks**
Big Foot
Black Mountain Rag
Boo Boo Stick Beat
Cannon Ball Rag
Country Gentleman
Dizzy Strings
Freight Train
Mister Sandman
Poor Boy Blues
Slinkey
Sneakin' Around
Trambone

# MUST SEE

It's always special to see a master in action, and some of the videos you can buy or view online of Chet in his vintage years are incredible. Here's a list of some must-see performances and instruction from Mr. Guitar both in DVD form and online on YouTube.

## On DVD

**Chet Atkins, Rare Performances (1955–1975)**, Vestapol

**Chet Atkins, Rare Performances (1976–1995)**, Vestapol

**Chet Atkins and Jerry Reed in Concert**, Vestapol

**The Guitar of Chet Atkins** (instructional video)

**Legends of Country Guitar**, Vestapol

Includes Chet Atkins, Merle Travis, Mose Rager, and Doc Watson

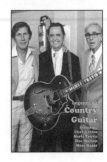

*Chet Atkins: Certified Guitar Player*

*Collection: Chet Atkins and Friends*

# On YouTube

### Mr. Sandman, Chet Atkins
This search should pull up a vintage (color) 1954 TV performance of Atkins playing "Mister Sandman."

### Entertainer, Chet Atkins
This search should find a 1975 clip of Atkins playing "The Entertainer" (taken from *The Legends of Country Guitar* listed previously).

### Black Mountain Rag, Chet Atkins
This should retrieve a vintage black-and-white performance of "Black Mountain Rag."

### Jerry's Breakdown
This 1975 performance on *Pop Goes Country* shows Chet Atkins and Jerry Reed in fine form picking "Jerry's Breakdown."

### Yakety Axe, Chet Atkins
This brings up quite a few live performances of Chet playing "Yakety Axe," and many are worth looking at. One of the best ones is a black-and-white performance from 1965 that you'll have to scroll down a bit to find.

### Galloping on the Guitar
This search brings up several great live videos of Chet performing the song—one with Mark O'Connor and another with Jethro Burns.

### Windy and Warm, Chet Atkins
Here's another search that pulls up several nice performances of Chet playing the song. One from "the early '60s" in black-and-white is particularly excellent.

### Wildwood Flower, Chet Atkins
This should retrieve several nice performances of "Wildwood Flower." Particularly excellent are the black-and-white 1960s TV performance and the 1950s colorized TV performance.

### Alabama Jubilee, Chet Atkins
This will retrieve a live performance of Chet Atkins playing with the Boston Pops, but the real gem is further down the page: a black-and-white performance with just band backing from 1956.

### Tiger Rag, Chet Atkins
Two great videos that come up with this search are an early 1960s TV performance and a live taping of Chet Atkins & the Blue Boys performing "Tiger Rag" along with "The Peanut Vendor" in Oslo, Norway.

# GUITAR *signature licks*

Signature Licks book/audio packs provide a step-by-step breakdown of "right from the record" riffs, licks, and solos so you can jam along with your favorite bands. They contain performance notes and an overview of each artist's or group's style, with note-for-note transcriptions in notes and tab. The online audio tracks feature full-band demos at both normal and slow speeds.

**AC/DC**
14041352 ...................... $22.99

**AEROSMITH 1973-1979**
00695106 ...................... $22.95

**AEROSMITH 1979-1998**
00695219 ...................... $22.95

**DUANE ALLMAN**
00696042 ...................... $22.99

**BEST OF CHET ATKINS**
00695752 ...................... $24.99

**AVENGED SEVENFOLD**
00696473 ...................... $22.99

**THE BEATLES**
00298845 ...................... $24.99

**BEST OF THE BEATLES FOR ACOUSTIC GUITAR**
00695453 ...................... $22.99

**THE BEATLES HITS**
00695049 ...................... $24.95

**JEFF BECK**
00696427 ...................... $22.99

**BEST OF GEORGE BENSON**
00695418 ...................... $22.99

**BEST OF BLACK SABBATH**
00695249 ...................... $22.95

**BLUES BREAKERS WITH JOHN MAYALL & ERIC CLAPTON**
00696374 ...................... $24.99

**BON JOVI**
00696380 ...................... $22.99

**ROY BUCHANAN**
00696654 ...................... $22.99

**KENNY BURRELL**
00695830 ...................... $24.99

**BEST OF CHARLIE CHRISTIAN**
00695584 ...................... $24.99

**BEST OF ERIC CLAPTON**
00695038 ...................... $24.99

**ERIC CLAPTON – FROM THE ALBUM UNPLUGGED**
00695250 ...................... $24.99

**BEST OF CREAM**
00695251 ...................... $22.95

**CREEDANCE CLEARWATER REVIVAL**
00695924 ...................... $24.99

**THE DOORS**
00695373 ...................... $22.95

**DEEP PURPLE – GREATEST HITS**
00695625 ...................... $22.99

**DREAM THEATER**
00111943 ...................... $24.99

**TOMMY EMMANUEL**
00696409 ...................... $22.99

**ESSENTIAL JAZZ GUITAR**
00695875 ...................... $19.99

**FAMOUS ROCK GUITAR SOLOS**
00695590 ...................... $19.95

**FLEETWOOD MAC**
00696416 ...................... $22.99

**BEST OF FOO FIGHTERS**
00695481 ...................... $24.95

**ROBBEN FORD**
00695903 ...................... $22.95

**BEST OF GRANT GREEN**
00695747 ...................... $22.99

**PETER GREEN**
00145386 ...................... $22.99

**BEST OF GUNS N' ROSES**
00695183 ...................... $24.99

**THE BEST OF BUDDY GUY**
00695186 ...................... $22.99

**JIM HALL**
00695848 ...................... $29.99

**JIMI HENDRIX**
00696560 ...................... $24.99

**JIMI HENDRIX – VOLUME 2**
00695835 ...................... $24.99

**JOHN LEE HOOKER**
00695894 ...................... $22.99

**BEST OF JAZZ GUITAR**
00695586 ...................... $29.99

**ERIC JOHNSON**
00699317 ...................... $24.99

**ROBERT JOHNSON**
00695264 ...................... $24.99

**BARNEY KESSEL**
00696009 ...................... $24.99

**THE ESSENTIAL ALBERT KING**
00695713 ...................... $24.99

**B.B. KING – BLUES LEGEND**
00696039 ...................... $22.99

**B.B. KING – THE DEFINITIVE COLLECTION**
00695635 ...................... $22.99

**MARK KNOPFLER**
00695178 ...................... $24.99

**LYNYRD SKYNYRD**
00695872 ...................... $24.99

**THE BEST OF YNGWIE MALMSTEEN**
00695669 ...................... $24.99

**BEST OF PAT MARTINO**
00695632 ...................... $24.99

**MEGADETH**
00696421 ...................... $22.99

**WES MONTGOMERY**
00695387 ...................... $24.99

**BEST OF NIRVANA**
00695483 ...................... $24.95

**VERY BEST OF OZZY OSBOURNE**
00695431 ...................... $22.99

**BRAD PAISLEY**
00696379 ...................... $22.99

**BEST OF JOE PASS**
00695730 ...................... $22.99

**TOM PETTY**
00696021 ...................... $22.99

**PINK FLOYD**
00103659 ...................... $24.99

**THE GUITAR OF ELVIS**
00174800 ...................... $22.99

**BEST OF QUEEN**
00695097 ...................... $24.99

**RADIOHEAD**
00109304 ...................... $24.99

**BEST OF RAGE AGAINST THE MACHINE**
00695480 ...................... $24.95

**RED HOT CHILI PEPPERS**
00695173 ...................... $22.95

**RED HOT CHILI PEPPERS – GREATEST HITS**
00695828 ...................... $24.99

**JERRY REED**
00118236 ...................... $22.99

**BEST OF DJANGO REINHARDT**
00695660 ...................... $24.99

**BEST OF ROCK 'N' ROLL GUITAR**
00695559 ...................... $22.99

**BEST OF ROCKABILLY GUITAR**
00695785 ...................... $19.99

**BEST OF CARLOS SANTANA**
00174664 ...................... $22.99

**BEST OF JOE SATRIANI**
00695216 ...................... $22.95

**SLASH**
00696576 ...................... $22.99

**SLAYER**
00121281 ...................... $22.99

**THE BEST OF SOUL GUITAR**
00695703 ...................... $19.95

**BEST OF SOUTHERN ROCK**
00695560 ...................... $19.95

**STEELY DAN**
00696015 ...................... $22.99

**MIKE STERN**
00695800 ...................... $24.99

**BEST OF SURF GUITAR**
00695822 ...................... $19.99

**STEVE VAI**
00673247 ...................... $24.99

**STEVE VAI – ALIEN LOVE SECRETS: THE NAKED VAMPS**
00695223 ...................... $22.95

**STEVE VAI – FIRE GARDEN: THE NAKED VAMPS**
00695166 ...................... $22.95

**STEVE VAI – THE ULTRA ZONE: NAKED VAMPS**
00695684 ...................... $22.95

**VAN HALEN**
00110227 ...................... $24.99

**STEVIE RAY VAUGHAN – 2ND ED.**
00699316 ...................... $24.95

**THE GUITAR STYLE OF STEVIE RAY VAUGHAN**
00695155 ...................... $24.95

**BEST OF THE VENTURES**
00695772 ...................... $19.95

**THE WHO – 2ND ED.**
00695561 ...................... $22.95

**JOHNNY WINTER**
00695951 ...................... $24.99

**YES**
00113120 ...................... $22.99

**NEIL YOUNG – GREATEST HITS**
00695988 ...................... $22.99

**BEST OF ZZ TOP**
00695738 ...................... $24.99

# HAL•LEONARD®

**www.halleonard.com**

**COMPLETE DESCRIPTIONS AND SONGLISTS ONLINE!**
Prices, contents and availability subject to change without notice.

# HAL•LEONARD® GUITAR PLAY-ALONG

This series will help you play your favorite songs quickly and easily. Just follow the tab and listen to the audio to the hear how the guitar should sound, and then play along using the separate backing tracks. Audio files also include software to slow down the tempo without changing pitch. The melody and lyrics are included in the book so that you can sing or simply follow along.

**INCLUDES TAB**

Complete song lists available online.

| | |
|---|---|
| VOL. 1 – ROCK | 00699570 / $16.99 |
| VOL. 2 – ACOUSTIC | 00699569 / $16.99 |
| VOL. 3 – HARD ROCK | 00699573 / $17.99 |
| VOL. 4 – POP/ROCK | 00699571 / $16.99 |
| VOL. 5 – THREE CHORD SONGS | 00300985 / $16.99 |
| VOL. 6 – '90S ROCK | 00298615 / $16.99 |
| VOL. 7 – BLUES | 00699575 / $17.99 |
| VOL. 8 – ROCK | 00699585 / $16.99 |
| VOL. 9 – EASY ACOUSTIC SONGS | 00151708 / $16.99 |
| VOL. 10 – ACOUSTIC | 00699586 / $16.95 |
| VOL. 11 – EARLY ROCK | 00699579 / $15.99 |
| VOL. 12 – ROCK POP | 00291724 / $16.99 |
| VOL. 14 – BLUES ROCK | 00699582 / $16.99 |
| VOL. 15 – R&B | 00699583 / $17.99 |
| VOL. 16 – JAZZ | 00699584 / $15.95 |
| VOL. 17 – COUNTRY | 00699588 / $16.99 |
| VOL. 18 – ACOUSTIC ROCK | 00699577 / $15.95 |
| VOL. 20 – ROCKABILLY | 00699580 / $16.99 |
| VOL. 21 – SANTANA | 00174525 / $17.99 |
| VOL. 22 – CHRISTMAS | 00699600 / $15.99 |
| VOL. 23 – SURF | 00699635 / $16.99 |
| VOL. 24 – ERIC CLAPTON | 00699649 / $17.99 |
| VOL. 25 – THE BEATLES | 00198265 / $17.99 |
| VOL. 26 – ELVIS PRESLEY | 00699643 / $16.99 |
| VOL. 27 – DAVID LEE ROTH | 00699645 / $16.95 |
| VOL. 28 – GREG KOCH | 00699646 / $17.99 |
| VOL. 29 – BOB SEGER | 00699647 / $16.99 |
| VOL. 30 – KISS | 00699644 / $16.99 |
| VOL. 32 – THE OFFSPRING | 00699653 / $14.95 |
| VOL. 33 – ACOUSTIC CLASSICS | 00699656 / $17.99 |
| VOL. 34 – CLASSIC ROCK | 00699658 / $17.99 |
| VOL. 35 – HAIR METAL | 00699660 / $17.99 |
| VOL. 36 – SOUTHERN ROCK | 00699661 / $19.99 |
| VOL. 37 – ACOUSTIC UNPLUGGED | 00699662 / $22.99 |
| VOL. 38 – BLUES | 00699663 / $17.99 |
| VOL. 39 – '80s METAL | 00699664 / $16.99 |
| VOL. 40 – INCUBUS | 00699668 / $17.95 |
| VOL. 41 – ERIC CLAPTON | 00699669 / $17.99 |
| VOL. 42 – COVER BAND HITS | 00211597 / $16.99 |
| VOL. 43 – LYNYRD SKYNYRD | 00699681 / $19.99 |
| VOL. 44 – JAZZ GREATS | 00699689 / $16.99 |
| VOL. 45 – TV THEMES | 00699718 / $14.95 |
| VOL. 46 – MAINSTREAM ROCK | 00699722 / $16.95 |
| VOL. 47 – JIMI HENDRIX SMASH HITS | 00699723 / $19.99 |
| VOL. 48 – AEROSMITH CLASSICS | 00699724 / $17.99 |
| VOL. 49 – STEVIE RAY VAUGHAN | 00699725 / $17.99 |
| VOL. 50 – VAN HALEN: 1978-1984 | 00110269 / $19.99 |
| VOL. 51 – ALTERNATIVE '90s | 00699727 / $14.99 |
| VOL. 52 – FUNK | 00699728 / $15.99 |
| VOL. 53 – DISCO | 00699729 / $14.99 |
| VOL. 54 – HEAVY METAL | 00699730 / $16.99 |
| VOL. 55 – POP METAL | 00699731 / $14.95 |
| VOL. 56 – FOO FIGHTERS | 00699749 / $17.99 |
| VOL. 57 – GUNS 'N' ROSES | 00159922 / $17.99 |
| VOL. 58 – BLINK 182 | 00699772 / $14.95 |
| VOL. 59 – CHET ATKINS | 00702347 / $16.99 |
| VOL. 60 – 3 DOORS DOWN | 00699774 / $14.95 |
| VOL. 62 – CHRISTMAS CAROLS | 00699798 / $12.95 |
| VOL. 63 – CREEDENCE CLEARWATER REVIVAL | 00699802 / $16.99 |
| VOL. 64 – ULTIMATE OZZY OSBOURNE | 00699803 / $17.99 |
| VOL. 66 – THE ROLLING STONES | 00699807 / $17.99 |
| VOL. 67 – BLACK SABBATH | 00699808 / $16.99 |
| VOL. 68 – PINK FLOYD – DARK SIDE OF THE MOON | 00699809 / $16.99 |
| VOL. 71 – CHRISTIAN ROCK | 00699824 / $14.95 |

| | |
|---|---|
| VOL. 72 – ACOUSTIC '90s | 00699827 / $14.95 |
| VOL. 73 – BLUESY ROCK | 00699829 / $16.99 |
| VOL. 74 – SIMPLE STRUMMING SONGS | 00151706 / $19.99 |
| VOL. 75 – TOM PETTY | 00699882 / $17.99 |
| VOL. 76 – COUNTRY HITS | 00699884 / $16.99 |
| VOL. 77 – BLUEGRASS | 00699910 / $15.99 |
| VOL. 78 – NIRVANA | 00700132 / $16.99 |
| VOL. 79 – NEIL YOUNG | 00700133 / $24.99 |
| VOL. 80 – ACOUSTIC ANTHOLOGY | 00700175 / $19.95 |
| VOL. 81 – ROCK ANTHOLOGY | 00700176 / $22.99 |
| VOL. 82 – EASY ROCK SONGS | 00700177 / $17.99 |
| VOL. 84 – STEELY DAN | 00700200 / $19.99 |
| VOL. 85 – THE POLICE | 00700269 / $16.99 |
| VOL. 86 – BOSTON | 00700465 / $16.99 |
| VOL. 87 – ACOUSTIC WOMEN | 00700763 / $14.99 |
| VOL. 88 – GRUNGE | 00700467 / $16.99 |
| VOL. 89 – REGGAE | 00700468 / $15.99 |
| VOL. 90 – CLASSICAL POP | 00700469 / $14.99 |
| VOL. 91 – BLUES INSTRUMENTALS | 00700505 / $17.99 |
| VOL. 92 – EARLY ROCK INSTRUMENTALS | 00700506 / $15.99 |
| VOL. 93 – ROCK INSTRUMENTALS | 00700507 / $16.99 |
| VOL. 94 – SLOW BLUES | 00700508 / $16.99 |
| VOL. 95 – BLUES CLASSICS | 00700509 / $15.99 |
| VOL. 96 – BEST COUNTRY HITS | 00211615 / $16.99 |
| VOL. 97 – CHRISTMAS CLASSICS | 00236542 / $14.99 |
| VOL. 98 – ROCK BAND | 00700704 / $14.95 |
| VOL. 99 – ZZ TOP | 00700762 / $16.99 |
| VOL. 100 – B.B. KING | 00700466 / $16.99 |
| VOL. 101 – SONGS FOR BEGINNERS | 00701917 / $14.99 |
| VOL. 102 – CLASSIC PUNK | 00700769 / $14.99 |
| VOL. 103 – SWITCHFOOT | 00700773 / $16.99 |
| VOL. 104 – DUANE ALLMAN | 00700846 / $17.99 |
| VOL. 105 – LATIN | 00700939 / $16.99 |
| VOL. 106 – WEEZER | 00700958 / $14.99 |
| VOL. 107 – CREAM | 00701069 / $16.99 |
| VOL. 108 – THE WHO | 00701053 / $16.99 |
| VOL. 109 – STEVE MILLER | 00701054 / $19.99 |
| VOL. 110 – SLIDE GUITAR HITS | 00701055 / $16.99 |
| VOL. 111 – JOHN MELLENCAMP | 00701056 / $14.99 |
| VOL. 112 – QUEEN | 00701052 / $16.99 |
| VOL. 113 – JIM CROCE | 00701058 / $17.99 |
| VOL. 114 – BON JOVI | 00701060 / $16.99 |
| VOL. 115 – JOHNNY CASH | 00701070 / $16.99 |
| VOL. 116 – THE VENTURES | 00701124 / $16.99 |
| VOL. 117 – BRAD PAISLEY | 00701224 / $16.99 |
| VOL. 118 – ERIC JOHNSON | 00701353 / $16.99 |
| VOL. 119 – AC/DC CLASSICS | 00701356 / $17.99 |
| VOL. 120 – PROGRESSIVE ROCK | 00701457 / $14.99 |
| VOL. 121 – U2 | 00701508 / $16.99 |
| VOL. 122 – CROSBY, STILLS & NASH | 00701610 / $16.99 |
| VOL. 123 – LENNON & McCARTNEY ACOUSTIC | 00701614 / $16.99 |
| VOL. 124 – SMOOTH JAZZ | 00200664 / $16.99 |
| VOL. 125 – JEFF BECK | 00701687 / $17.99 |
| VOL. 126 – BOB MARLEY | 00701701 / $16.99 |
| VOL. 127 – 1970s ROCK | 00701739 / $16.99 |
| VOL. 128 – 1960s ROCK | 00701740 / $14.99 |
| VOL. 129 – MEGADETH | 00701741 / $17.99 |
| VOL. 130 – IRON MAIDEN | 00701742 / $17.99 |
| VOL. 131 – 1990s ROCK | 00701743 / $14.99 |
| VOL. 132 – COUNTRY ROCK | 00701757 / $15.99 |
| VOL. 133 – TAYLOR SWIFT | 00701894 / $16.99 |
| VOL. 134 – AVENGED SEVENFOLD | 00701906 / $16.99 |
| VOL. 135 – MINOR BLUES | 00151350 / $17.99 |
| VOL. 136 – GUITAR THEMES | 00701922 / $14.99 |
| VOL. 137 – IRISH TUNES | 00701966 / $15.99 |
| VOL. 138 – BLUEGRASS CLASSICS | 00701967 / $17.99 |

| | |
|---|---|
| VOL. 139 – GARY MOORE | 00702370 / $16.99 |
| VOL. 140 – MORE STEVIE RAY VAUGHAN | 00702396 / $17.99 |
| VOL. 141 – ACOUSTIC HITS | 00702401 / $16.99 |
| VOL. 142 – GEORGE HARRISON | 00237697 / $17.99 |
| VOL. 143 – SLASH | 00702425 / $19.99 |
| VOL. 144 – DJANGO REINHARDT | 00702531 / $16.99 |
| VOL. 145 – DEF LEPPARD | 00702532 / $17.99 |
| VOL. 146 – ROBERT JOHNSON | 00702533 / $16.99 |
| VOL. 147 – SIMON & GARFUNKEL | 14041591 / $16.99 |
| VOL. 148 – BOB DYLAN | 14041592 / $16.99 |
| VOL. 149 – AC/DC HITS | 14041593 / $17.99 |
| VOL. 150 – ZAKK WYLDE | 02501717 / $16.99 |
| VOL. 151 – J.S. BACH | 02501730 / $16.99 |
| VOL. 152 – JOE BONAMASSA | 02501751 / $19.99 |
| VOL. 153 – RED HOT CHILI PEPPERS | 00702990 / $19.99 |
| VOL. 154 – GLEE | 00703018 / $16.99 |
| VOL. 155 – ERIC CLAPTON UNPLUGGED | 00703085 / $16.99 |
| VOL. 156 – SLAYER | 00703770 / $19.99 |
| VOL. 157 – FLEETWOOD MAC | 00101382 / $17.99 |
| VOL. 159 – WES MONTGOMERY | 00102593 / $19.99 |
| VOL. 160 – T-BONE WALKER | 00102641 / $17.99 |
| VOL. 161 – THE EAGLES ACOUSTIC | 00102659 / $17.99 |
| VOL. 162 – THE EAGLES HITS | 00102667 / $17.99 |
| VOL. 163 – PANTERA | 00103036 / $17.99 |
| VOL. 164 – VAN HALEN: 1986-1995 | 00110270 / $17.99 |
| VOL. 165 – GREEN DAY | 00210343 / $17.99 |
| VOL. 166 – MODERN BLUES | 00700764 / $16.99 |
| VOL. 167 – DREAM THEATER | 00111938 / $24.99 |
| VOL. 168 – KISS | 00113421 / $17.99 |
| VOL. 169 – TAYLOR SWIFT | 00115982 / $16.99 |
| VOL. 170 – THREE DAYS GRACE | 00117337 / $16.99 |
| VOL. 171 – JAMES BROWN | 00117420 / $16.99 |
| VOL. 172 – THE DOOBIE BROTHERS | 00119670 / $16.99 |
| VOL. 173 – TRANS-SIBERIAN ORCHESTRA | 00119907 / $19.99 |
| VOL. 174 – SCORPIONS | 00122119 / $16.99 |
| VOL. 175 – MICHAEL SCHENKER | 00122127 / $17.99 |
| VOL. 176 – BLUES BREAKERS WITH JOHN MAYALL & ERIC CLAPTON | 00122132 / $19.99 |
| VOL. 177 – ALBERT KING | 00123271 / $16.99 |
| VOL. 178 – JASON MRAZ | 00124165 / $17.99 |
| VOL. 179 – RAMONES | 00127073 / $16.99 |
| VOL. 180 – BRUNO MARS | 00129706 / $16.99 |
| VOL. 181 – JACK JOHNSON | 00129854 / $16.99 |
| VOL. 182 – SOUNDGARDEN | 00138161 / $17.99 |
| VOL. 183 – BUDDY GUY | 00138240 / $17.99 |
| VOL. 184 – KENNY WAYNE SHEPHERD | 00138258 / $17.99 |
| VOL. 185 – JOE SATRIANI | 00139457 / $17.99 |
| VOL. 186 – GRATEFUL DEAD | 00139459 / $17.99 |
| VOL. 187 – JOHN DENVER | 00140839 / $17.99 |
| VOL. 188 – MÖTLEY CRÜE | 00141145 / $17.99 |
| VOL. 189 – JOHN MAYER | 00144350 / $17.99 |
| VOL. 190 – DEEP PURPLE | 00146152 / $17.99 |
| VOL. 191 – PINK FLOYD CLASSICS | 00146164 / $17.99 |
| VOL. 192 – JUDAS PRIEST | 00151352 / $17.99 |
| VOL. 193 – STEVE VAI | 00156028 / $19.99 |
| VOL. 194 – PEARL JAM | 00157925 / $17.99 |
| VOL. 195 – METALLICA: 1983-1988 | 00234291 / $19.99 |
| VOL. 196 – METALLICA: 1991-2016 | 00234292 / $19.99 |

*Prices, contents, and availability subject to change without notice.*

## HAL•LEONARD®
www.halleonard.com

0820

# Get Better at Guitar

## ...with these Great Guitar Instruction Books from Hal Leonard!

### 101 GUITAR TIPS
INCLUDES TAB

STUFF ALL THE PROS KNOW AND USE

*by Adam St. James*

This book contains invaluable guidance on everything from scales and music theory to truss rod adjustments, proper recording studio set-ups, and much more. The book also features snippets of advice from some of the most celebrated guitarists and producers in the music business, including B.B. King, Steve Vai, Joe Satriani, Warren Haynes, Laurence Juber, Pete Anderson, Tom Dowd and others, culled from the author's hundreds of interviews.

00695737 Book/Online Audio ..................$16.99

### AMAZING PHRASING
INCLUDES TAB

50 WAYS TO IMPROVE YOUR IMPROVISATIONAL SKILLS

*by Tom Kolb*

This book/audio pack explores all the main components necessary for crafting well-balanced rhythmic and melodic phrases. It also explains how these phrases are put together to form cohesive solos. Many styles are covered – rock, blues, jazz, fusion, country, Latin, funk and more – and all of the concepts are backed up with musical examples. The companion audio contains 89 demos for listening, and most tracks feature full-band backing.

00695583 Book/Online Audio ..................$19.99

### BLUES YOU CAN USE – 2ND EDITION

*by John Ganapes*

This comprehensive source for learning blues guitar is designed to develop both your lead and rhythm playing. Includes: 21 complete solos • blues chords, progressions and riffs • turnarounds • movable scales and soloing techniques • string bending • utilizing the entire fingerboard • and more. This second edition now includes audio and video access online!

00142420 Book/Online Media..................$19.99

### FRETBOARD MASTERY
INCLUDES TAB

*by Troy Stetina*

Untangle the mysterious regions of the guitar fretboard and unlock your potential. *Fretboard Mastery* familiarizes you with all the shapes you need to know by applying them in real musical examples, thereby reinforcing and reaffirming your newfound knowledge. The result is a much higher level of comprehension and retention.

00695331 Book/Online Audio ..................$19.99

### FRETBOARD ROADMAPS – 2ND EDITION

ESSENTIAL GUITAR PATTERNS THAT ALL THE PROS KNOW AND USE

*by Fred Sokolow*

The updated edition of this bestseller features more songs, updated lessons, audio tracks! Learn to play lead and rhythm anywhere on the fretboard, in any key; play a variety of lead guitar styles; play chords and progressions anywhere on the fretboard; expand your chord vocabulary; and learn to think musically – the way the pros do.

00695941 Book/Online Audio ..................$15.99

### GUITAR AEROBICS
INCLUDES TAB

A 52-WEEK, ONE-LICK-PER-DAY WORKOUT PROGRAM FOR DEVELOPING, IMPROVING & MAINTAINING GUITAR TECHNIQUE

*by Troy Nelson*

From the former editor of *Guitar One* magazine, here is a daily dose of vitamins to keep your chops fine tuned! Musical styles include rock, blues, jazz, metal, country, and funk. Techniques taught include alternate picking, arpeggios, sweep picking, string skipping, legato, string bending, and rhythm guitar. These exercises will increase speed, and improve dexterity and pick- and fret-hand accuracy. The accompanying audio includes all 365 workout licks plus play-along grooves in every style at eight different metronome settings.

00695946 Book/Online Audio ..................$19.99

### GUITAR CLUES
INCLUDES TAB

OPERATION PENTATONIC

*by Greg Koch*

Join renowned guitar master Greg Koch as he clues you in to a wide variety of fun and valuable pentatonic scale applications. Whether you're new to improvising or have been doing it for a while, this book/audio pack will provide loads of delicious licks and tricks that you can use right away, from volume swells and chicken pickin' to intervallic and chordal ideas. The online audio includes 65 demo and play-along tracks.

00695827 Book/Online Audio ..................$19.99

### INTRODUCTION TO GUITAR TONE & EFFECTS

*by David M. Brewster*

This book/audio pack teaches the basics of guitar tones and effects, with online audio examples. Readers will learn about: overdrive, distortion and fuzz • using equalizers • modulation effects • reverb and delay • multi-effect processors • and more.

00695766 Book/Online Audio ..................$16.99

### PICTURE CHORD ENCYCLOPEDIA

This comprehensive guitar chord resource for all playing styles and levels features five voicings of 44 chord qualities for all twelve keys – 2,640 chords in all! For each, there is a clearly illustrated chord frame, as well as *an actual photo* of the chord being played! Includes info on basic fingering principles, open chords and barre chords, partial chords and broken-set forms, and more.

00695224................................................$19.95

### SCALE CHORD RELATIONSHIPS
INCLUDES TAB

*by Michael Mueller & Jeff Schroedl*

This book teaches players how to determine which scales to play with which chords, so guitarists will never have to fear chord changes again! This book/audio pack explains how to: recognize keys • analyze chord progressions • use the modes • play over nondiatonic harmony • use harmonic and melodic minor scales • use symmetrical scales such as chromatic, whole-tone and diminished scales • incorporate exotic scales such as Hungarian major and Gypsy minor • and much more!

00695563 Book/Online Audio ..................$14.99

### SPEED MECHANICS FOR LEAD GUITAR
INCLUDES TAB

Take your playing to the stratosphere with the most advanced lead book by this proven heavy metal author. *Speed Mechanics* is the ultimate technique book for developing the kind of speed and precision in today's explosive playing styles. Learn the fastest ways to achieve speed and control, secrets to make your practice time really count, and how to open your ears and make your musical ideas more solid and tangible. Packed with over 200 vicious exercises including Troy's scorching version of "Flight of the Bumblebee." Music and examples demonstrated on the accompanying online audio.

00699323 Book/Online Audio ..................$19.99

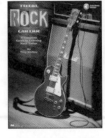

### TOTAL ROCK GUITAR
INCLUDES TAB

A COMPLETE GUIDE TO LEARNING ROCK GUITAR

*by Troy Stetina*

This unique and comprehensive source for learning rock guitar is designed to develop both lead and rhythm playing. It covers: getting a tone that rocks • open chords, power chords and barre chords • riffs, scales and licks • string bending, strumming, palm muting, harmonics and alternate picking • all rock styles • and much more. The examples are in standard notation with chord grids and tab, and the audio includes full-band backing for all 22 songs.

00695246 Book/Online Audio ..................$19.99

Visit Hal Leonard Online at
**www.halleonard.com**

## HAL•LEONARD®